Mountain
Kids

Linda Goyette

Happy reading!
Linda Goyette

BRINDLE
&GLASS

Library and Archives Canada Cataloguing in Publication
Goyette, Linda, 1955–
Rocky Mountain kids / Linda Goyette

ISBN 978-1-897142-32-5

1. Rocky Mountains, Canadian (B.C. and Alta.)—History—Juvenile literature.
2. Children—Rocky Mountains, Canadian—History—Juvenile literature.
3. Children—Rocky Mountains, Canadian—Biography—Juvenile literature. I. Title.

PS8613.O985R63 2008   j971.1   C2007-907438-3

Library of Congress Control Number: 2008921086

Cover design: Frances Hunter
Cover image: Tobyn Manthorpe, inspired by Whyte Museum Archives image V683-111.F.1.
Map: Wendy Johnson, Johnson Cartographers
Author photo: AlbertaViews

 Canada Council   Conseil des Arts
for the Arts   du Canada
 Canadian   Patrimoine
Heritage   canadien

Brindle & Glass acknowledges the support of the Canada Council for the Arts, and the Government of Canada through the Book Publishing Industry Development Program (BPIDP) for their contributions to our publishing program.

Brindle & Glass Publishing
www.brindleandglass.com

To Kira and Peter, who love the mountains too.

The Stories

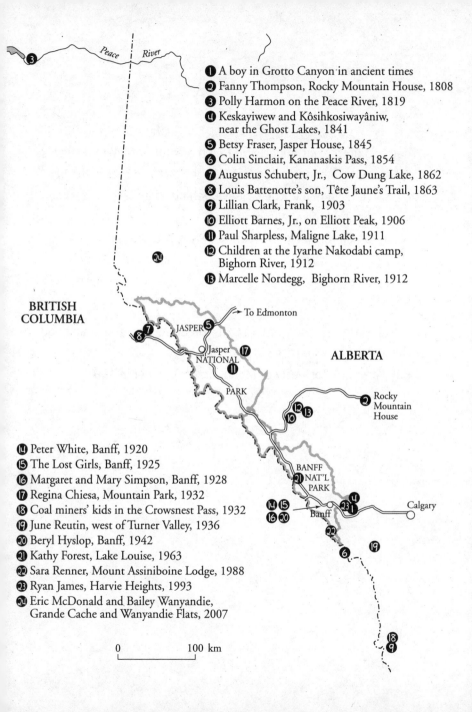

1. A boy in Grotto Canyon in ancient times
2. Fanny Thompson, Rocky Mountain House, 1808
3. Polly Harmon on the Peace River, 1819
4. Keskayiwew and Kôsihkosiwayâniw, near the Ghost Lakes, 1841
5. Betsy Fraser, Jasper House, 1845
6. Colin Sinclair, Kananaskis Pass, 1854
7. Augustus Schubert, Jr., Cow Dung Lake, 1862
8. Louis Battenotte's son, Tête Jaune's Trail, 1863
9. Lillian Clark, Frank, 1903
10. Elliott Barnes, Jr., on Elliott Peak, 1906
11. Paul Sharpless, Maligne Lake, 1911
12. Children at the Iyarhe Nakodabi camp, Bighorn River, 1912
13. Marcelle Nordegg, Bighorn River, 1912
14. Peter White, Banff, 1920
15. The Lost Girls, Banff, 1925
16. Margaret and Mary Simpson, Banff, 1928
17. Regina Chiesa, Mountain Park, 1932
18. Coal miners' kids in the Crowsnest Pass, 1932
19. June Reutin, west of Turner Valley, 1936
20. Beryl Hyslop, Banff, 1942
21. Kathy Forest, Lake Louise, 1963
22. Sara Renner, Mount Assiniboine Lodge, 1988
23. Ryan James, Harvie Heights, 1993
24. Eric McDonald and Bailey Wanyandie, Grande Cache and Wanyandie Flats, 2007

Peace River

BRITISH COLUMBIA

ALBERTA

To Edmonton

JASPER

Jasper NATIONAL

PARK

Rocky Mountain House

BANFF NAT'L PARK

Banff

Calgary

0   100 km

"They had better not mine Third Hill: that's for sure. When I was a girl, I pounded a handmade cross into the dirt and rocks, and I put some salami inside a bottle to leave behind as a marker. I claimed that hill for Queen Isabella of Spain."
—Gloria Dagil, formerly of Mountain Park, Alberta, 1997

We had a tremendous amount of freedom, and fun and good times. Oh, to feel that free in a lifetime!
—Kay Farnham, formerly of Mountain Park, Alberta, 1997

Introduction
A promise to readers

I have always been curious about the Canadian kids who are lucky enough to live in the Rocky Mountains. Several years ago, I began to collect their stories for this book. You might like to know how I did it.

First, I talked to Alberta kids who live in the mountains today, and to older people who lived there when they were young. I asked permission to publish their stories. If they said yes, I wrote down their exact words in my notebook. Then I went home and created a story. I asked each storyteller to check the story so it would be as true as possible.

Later, I began to hunt for the interesting kids who explored the Rockies in the distant past. They died long ago, of course, so it was impossible to talk to them. How could I find out what they did, and what they were thinking as they explored the mountains?

Hunting for their lost stories became a game of hide and seek. I searched for clues about forgotten kids in Canada's libraries, archives, and museums. I opened old history books and diaries, and listened carefully for the echoes of giggles as I turned the musty pages.

Rocky Mountain kids sprang from hidden corners of Canadian history—waving at me from a distance—but they couldn't talk to me. I could learn their names and investigate their lives, but I found no words that they had spoken when they were young.

This left me wondering what to do. When writers invent

words for real people in another century, or in another culture, we are bound to get the story wrong. Wild guesses can be fun, but they do not add up to the truth. When writing about real people, we have to be careful with the truth.

I could have written about imaginary characters, but I wanted you to meet the living, breathing kids of the past. They had important stories to tell and they needed somebody to listen. I wanted you to hear them talking to you, asking you questions, and calling to you to follow them up over rocks, and up steep trails.

The first kids in the Rockies were interesting people. How can we get to know them if we don't try to hear their voices with our imaginations?

Thinking it over, I decided to make you a promise.

I promise that every named child or teenager in this book is a real person who once camped or lived in the Canadian Rockies. After each story, I will tell you what I know is true, and also what details I imagined. You will find the truth in each story, hiding behind the guesses.

Maybe you will wonder why some kids in the early stories have English names even thought they were First Nations or Métis children who spoke other languages in their everyday life. In the early years of western Canada, many kids grew up with a name in their tribal language along with a name in English or French. Sometimes only their English or French names were written down, so that is all we know today.

Children who lived in the Rockies—in the past, and today—speak the languages of the world, not only English. I used some words of their first languages in these stories so you could hear and say them. You will find a list of special Rocky Mountain words at the back of the book.

Few people in western Canada had cameras when the first kids travelled in the Rockies so you will find no photographs of them in the early stories. You will have to use your imagination to see their faces.

If you don't mind, I will try to imagine you, too. Will you read these stories beside a campfire in Canada, or under the blankets with a flashlight in a bed in Brazil? On a front porch somewhere in the United States? On a picnic in India? On a bus in Nigeria? On a balcony in Japan? On a train in Germany? In a big, soft chair in China? Will someone read this book aloud to you so you can close your eyes and imagine that you are on a high trail in the mountains with new friends? I hope so.

The Rocky Mountains in Canada belong to all human beings, including you. I hope you will explore them for yourself someday. You can write your story down, or tell it to somebody, but living it is what matters most. Happy exploring.

Linda Goyette

Edmonton, Alberta, Canada

2008

Day of the cougar

A boy in Grotto Canyon, age eight,
on an unknown day in ancient times

Touch the bumps along your spine with your fingertip. Can you feel them?

The Rocky Mountains are the backbone of the world. Maybe you live near the top of the world, between the shoulders of North America. You call this place Canada. That word does not exist in my language.

My clan came from a place near the fat belly of our continent. I can't tell you when our journey began. I was born somewhere along the way.

My mother said she stopped to rest under a tree one summer morning, and found a hiccupping baby, lying on a flat stone beside a creek.

"That was you," she said. "You looked like a turtle."

She said she decided to keep me because she likes turtles. "I picked you up from the rock, and you got scared, and disappeared right back into your shell," she said. "It was six months before I saw your face again."

I'm not sure I believe this story. She was smiling in a funny way when she said it.

We have been following these mountains for as long as I can remember—walking and walking—just to see how far up the world they go.

This is not our territory, so we have to be careful. The people who belong here might not like us. They speak a different language from us. They dress in different clothes. We are hunting for the same large elk they need for their food, and they might not like that either. I'm afraid they will find us and start a war with us, and what will happen to us then?

We make our night camps in places where nobody can see us. The old people keep the cooking fire small and low, and they tell us stories in whispers about the magical creatures and giant beasts that live in the highest places in the mountains.

This territory is shiver-cold at night. Wolves and coyotes howl. Owls shriek from twisted branches. While others sleep, I stare into the darkness with my eyes wide open. Outside the lodge, wild animals seem to be telling me: "Go away, young stranger. You belong in the place where the ice never goes."

In the morning, when I am sleepy after a scary night, my older brothers and sisters sneak up behind me to snarl like cougars. If I jump, they fall down, roll around on the ground, and hold their stomachs while they laugh themselves silly.

Yesterday, when my older sister said I had the courage of a chickadee, I decided to get even with all of them.

I left our camp to explore the narrow, rocky cliffs in a canyon not too far away, and I made my plan.

"I saw a cougar today," I told my big brothers and sisters when I came back. "Her teeth were sharper than arrows. Her claws were longer than spear points."

They looked at me, and rolled their eyes. I didn't let their snickers bother me.

"Would you like to see the cougar? I can take you to her den tomorrow."

They started to laugh at me again. "How do you know your big cougar will still be waiting for you?"

I could tell they didn't believe me.

"Come and see for yourself," I said. I shrugged, then walked away.

This afternoon they followed me to the canyon. I guess they had nothing better to do. We walked beside a creek in a thick forest until we reached the cliffs.

"Let's hide here so we can watch the cougar feed her babies," I told them. We climbed up to some high boulders, crouched behind them, and waited. In a few minutes, the afternoon sun made a big scary shadow on the smooth cliff, and it looked like . . .

"A cougar!" yelled my oldest brother. He scrambled away. All of my brothers and sisters ran after him, screeching and hollering so loudly that I could hear their echoes through the canyon.

I sat in my hiding place, smiling at my trick. They would never laugh at me again, those chickadees. In my quiet spot, out of the wind, I soon fell fast asleep. When I woke up, I peeked over the boulder to check for a cougar that wasn't a shadow.

I saw that I was not alone. A tall man walked slowly toward the cliff. Could it be an enemy with a spear? Would he hurt me? My heart pounded like a drum in my chest.

I looked closer, and saw that the man was my grandfather.

He began to draw a picture on the rock with red mud. I could see he was drawing the shape of Maahu, the curved-back man who plays the flute, the sign of our clan.

I stayed in my hiding place, peeking through the rocks. Would he be angry with me for watching him? I wasn't sure. When he finished the drawing, he wiped his hands and walked back to our camp. I followed him. I think he knew I was behind him, but he said nothing.

"This part of the world is too cold for us," my grandfather told our family tonight. "We have made our mark here. Tomorrow we will turn around, and follow these mountains back to the place where we began."

Tomorrow I will begin my long walk home.

What do we know for sure?

We will never know the names of the first kids who came to the northern Rockies—or their true cougar stories—but their families did leave behind many rock drawings.

I imagined this story as if it happened in Grotto Canyon, just west of Calgary. If you follow Highway 1A, you will reach the Grotto Mountain picnic area. You can follow the Grotto Creek Trail through the woods into the canyon, and search for the picture of the curved-back man playing a flute. It is very hard to see, but it is there.

Nobody knows exactly who drew this picture. In her book *Stone by Stone: Exploring Ancient Sites on the Canadian Plains*, Liz Bryan offers one interesting idea. The Hopi people in the United States tell an old, old story about the members of the Flute Clan, who travelled north along the edge of the mountains until they reached a place covered with snow and ice. It was too cold for them, so they decided to turn around and go south again. They drew a picture of their Maahu, the flute-playing man, on a cliff to leave their mark.

Liz Bryan's book is full of beautiful pictures of the stone carvings, rock art, buffalo jumps, and buffalo rubbing stones of the people of the First Nations in ancient times—including five special places in the Rockies. Human beings have been exploring these mountains for thousands of years. Archaeologists have found the oldest campsite at Vermilion Lakes, under Mount Rundle near Banff, where people camped 10,800 years ago.

As for cougars, they do live in the Canadian Rockies today, but they are so shy that they rarely show themselves to humans. Other wild cats in the mountains include the lynx and the bobcat.

My squirmy little brother

Fanny Thompson, age seven,
Rocky Mountain House, Rupert's Land, 1808

I rode across the Rocky Mountains on a horse when I was six years old.

Don't look so surprised. I rode back again when I was seven. I was not one bit scared.

The hard part was holding on to Samuel, my three-year-old brother. He sat in front of me on my horse for hours every day. My mother told me it was my job to keep him safe, but she kept her eye on us every minute.

That boy squirmed, twisted, and wriggled to get away from my arms. When I held him tighter, he pushed me backward and sideways with his pudgy hands. When our horse climbed up a steep trail, I worried he would tumble off and fall into the canyon—pulling me down with him.

"Stop wiggling!" I ordered. He looked at me and laughed his head off.

Do you have a squirmy little brother? Maybe you know how I feel.

My horse understood little boys. I called her *pakwatastim*, my good horse. She carried us up, up, up on narrow rocky trails, and down, down, down on twisting, rocky ridges. My horse didn't jump when Samuel pulled her mane or put his fingers in her ears. She didn't toss us off her back when spruce branches slapped her face, or when hundreds of mosquitoes bit her rump.

I loved *pakwatastim* because she helped me put up with Samuel. She also carried heavy saddlebags packed with our blankets, warm clothes, and extra moccasins.

Ahead of me, my mother rode a bigger horse loaded down with heavy bags of pemmican, tea, and cooking pots. She pulled my horse with a gentle lead. As she rode, my mother carried my baby sister, Emma, on her back. When Emma was hungry, my mother could feed her without stopping.

Do you wonder why we travel so much?

My father is searching for a river that will guide fur traders to the Pacific Ocean. He makes maps of the land, maps of the mountains, and maps of the stars in the sky.

"You can help me, Fanny," he says. "You can count the tops of the mountains that we pass."

That's why I am always looking up at the sky, and all around in a circle.

In the spring, we left Rocky Mountain House, the trading post where I was born. Lots of people travelled with us. I counted nine kids, five mothers, and thirteen men.

Our travelling days were long and hard. We crossed rushing creeks with the water up to the horses' knees. Our horses stumbled in sticky muck and fell into deep holes. Riding into one forest after a wildfire, *pakwatastim* tripped over burnt trees that had tumbled to the ground. Whenever my horse fell down, Samuel and I fell too.

Samuel cried with his mouth wide open. Each time he would gulp down a cloud of mosquitoes by mistake. That made him howl even louder, especially if he was hungry for something that tasted good.

Wolverine the Hunter brought us two horse-loads of deer meat, and other hunters brought us buffalo meat and sometimes porcupine. Soon we were riding through meadows filled with saskatoon berries. When we saw glaciers, we turned toward the mountains.

We climbed and climbed on horseback. Snow surrounded us, and finally stopped us. "We can't climb higher until it melts," my father said. For fourteen days, we stayed in our camp, waiting for the summer sun to help us.

One warm day, we started to climb again. Soon we reached the highest lookout in the pass. I stood on the top of the world, counting peaks.

"Look down, Fanny," my father said. "This is where all the little rivers run away to the sea."

I tried to look down, but it made me dizzy.

It was time to go down to the other side of the mountains. My mother lifted Samuel and me back onto *pakwatastim*'s wide back. For the next five days, our family zigzagged down a dangerous trail along a narrow ridge of rock.

Our horses fell many times. We crossed flooded streams so deep that my father and the other men struggled to guide our horses across to the far shore. I could feel Samuel shiver through his cold, wet shirt.

I couldn't let him go, or he might drown.

I gave my brother a lump of sugar to keep him still. When he gulped that down, I pointed to birds, rabbits, and deer on the far shore.

"Count them!" I ordered.

Samuel can only count to three, so that plan didn't work. I told him stories about little people who live in the mountains. For a few minutes, he didn't move a muscle.

Suddenly, the trail stopped. Grown-ups had to hack down trees with axes so we could find our way through the forest. At last we saw a river in the distance. My father and the other men made canoes out of birch trees, and carried us to our places in them. Samuel and I sat together, squeezed between big sacks of pemmican, as the men paddled our canoe into a wide lake. My brother tried to climb out of the canoe, but I stopped him.

I kept asking my mother the same question: "When are we going to get there?"

"Soon," she said, a thousand times.

At last my family found a stopping place. We climbed out of the canoe, and all the mothers set up the camp. We had run out of food, and we were so hungry. We got sick eating the last sour, bad meat, but the Kootenay people who came to our camp gave us wild meat and berries to make us feel better.

"We will build a trading post here where we can stay warm this winter," my father said. Five men worked hard to build a two-room log house for us. One room was for our family, and one room was for trading furs with the Kootenay hunters. The windows had a skin, as thin as paper, to let the sunlight come in.

"This will be your sleeping place, Fanny," my mother said. She pointed to a pile of warm blankets near the stone fireplace.

When the fall came, the men built a high log wall around our house to protect us in case the Pikani people and the Kootenay people had a war. We could climb up a ladder to the top to watch the woods for strangers.

"Now that everything is finished, I can leave you here while I go exploring," my father said. "I will come back for you in the spring."

We stayed at Kootenay House through the long, cold winter—all the mothers, the children, and three men. At night we listened to wolves and coyotes howling at the moon. In the mornings, our mothers walked on snowshoes to snare rabbits and wood grouse for our stew.

They are good hunters, but it was a hungry winter. Our friends, the Kootenay hunters, could not find enough big animals to feed everyone, and we slowly ran out of every bit of pemmican and tea. Sometimes my empty stomach ached. I am sad to say we had to eat some sled dogs to survive.

Finally, my mother said we could not wait for my father one minute longer. "We are almost starving," she told the men. "We have to go back home." Finan McDonald, Clement, and Bercier packed up our horses for the trip back over the mountains to our home country.

Galloping on horseback, my father caught up with us a few days after we left Kootenay House.

That should have been a happy time, but everything went wrong. Samuel and I were riding a big new horse. The new horse was nervous and jumpy. He slipped sideways on some rocks, and when the saddlebags fell off, he bucked and reared up as we struggled to hang on.

My father wanted to save Samuel and me, and he thought that the new horse was sick and dangerous. He shot the horse with his rifle while we were still on the big animal's back. We were so surprised! We tumbled to the ground.

That was a terrible day, but not the worst one. One afternoon, a few days later, my little sister Emma got lost.

We were camping high in the mountains. Emma was two years old by then, and too curious. My mother turned her back just for a minute, when she was packing up the horses, and my little sister crept away into the woods.

We ran in all directions, terrified, calling her name. Had Emma drowned in the river? We searched the rapids, and the darkest places in the woods, for five hours. Even Samuel joined the hunt. We almost gave up hope.

"Here, I've found her footprints!" Finan shouted at last.

We followed the little tracks, and found Emma sleeping against a snowdrift.

Lifting her gently, my father put my little sister in my mother's arms, and said: "You are so brave, Charlotte, but I know you and the children have suffered on this trip. Let's head for Rocky Mountain House."

We rode down our side of the mountains to Saskatchewan Crossing, and then paddled on the North Saskatchewan River to the little fur-trading post where my cousins waited. Two months later, my mother gave us a new baby brother named John.

"Soon you can ride with him, too," she said with a smile.

Maybe, but I think my Rocky Mountain riding days are almost over. My family is moving to Fort Augustus soon, but I will travel by canoe on the rivers across the plains to a big city in the east.

Soon I will be eight. My parents are sending me to school in Montreal, and my mother said she will miss me every minute I'm away.

"You will learn to speak and write in English and French, but when you dream of us in the mountains, you will dream in Cree," she told me. "You will count tall buildings instead of mountains, rivers, and stars."

Will Samuel miss me? I think he will.

What do we know for sure?

Fanny Thompson was born at the fur-trading post of Rocky Mountain House, on June 10, 1801.

Fanny travelled through the Rocky Mountains, the forests, and the plains with her parents from the time she was born until she was eight years old. Her squirmy little brother, Samuel, was born at Peace River. Like many children in fur-trading families, Fanny and Samuel spoke Cree, French, and English.

Fanny's father, David Thompson, was Canada's most famous map-maker. He grew up in London, England. When he was only fourteen years old, he became an apprentice for the Hudson's Bay Company. He travelled across the Atlantic Ocean in a big ship to work in Rupert's Land, the old name for western Canada. He started to work as a fur trader for the North West Company when he was twenty-seven years old.

Fanny's mother, Charlotte Small, was born in the West, long before Canada became a country. She spoke Cree and grew up with her Cree relatives, although her father was a Scottish fur trader.

David and Charlotte met at Ile La Crosse, in what is now northern Saskatchewan. Charlotte was not quite fourteen years old when she became David's wife. They lived together for the rest of their lives. They had at least twelve children, maybe fourteen, but some of their sons and daughters died when they were little.

The story about Fanny's two difficult trips through the Rockies is true. Her father kept a record in his diary. On June 19, 1808, David Thompson wrote about shooting the horse that Fanny and Samuel were riding. "One of my horses nearly crushing my children to death from his load being badly put on, which I mistook for being vicious; I shot him on the spot and rescued my little ones." He also wrote about the search for the lost little Emma the next day.

In those days, children often died of diseases when they were small. Fanny's new baby brother, John—described by his father as "a beautiful, promising boy"—died when he was five years old. Emma died a month later at the age of seven years. Her sad father said she was "an amiable, innocent little girl, too good for this world."

And Fanny? She grew up and lived to be a healthy old woman. She lived in Williamstown, Ontario, and Montreal, and died in 1884 at the age of eighty-three.

If you travel in western Canada, you can visit some of the places in Fanny's story.

Fanny started her difficult trip at Rocky Mountain House, her birthplace, which is now a friendly town in central Alberta. She rode into the wild territory that is now Banff National Park. Travelling with six horses, the family followed the Blaeberry River and crossed the high mountains through the Howse Pass. They came down narrow, difficult trails into the forests around the present-day town of Golden, BC.

Fanny spent her hard winter at Kootenay House, near today's town of Invermere, BC. Her family used the English word Kootenay to describe the local people who helped them so much. They call themselves the Ktunaxa Nation (pronounced k-too-nah-ha). You can learn more about their history, and their community in British Columbia today, at the web site www.ktunaxa.org

Fanny's family returned over the mountains to meet their relatives at a small trading post. Later they moved to a fur-trading post called Fort Augustus, in the place we now know as Edmonton, Alberta. Today, baseball players hit home runs, and crowds cheer for them, at Telus Field in the river valley—in the same place where Fanny once played with her brother.

Trouble!

Polly Harmon, age eight,
in a canoe on the Peace River, May 1819

I think I am going to drown. Let me change that. I know I am going to drown!

Our canoe is tipping, side to side, and I know it will dump all of us into this angry, nasty river before the end of the day. Who decided to call it the Peace River? What is so peaceful about it?

Ice-cold water is splashing across my face. My lips and eyelids are numb. I am soaked from the top of my head to the toes of my moccasins. Can you hear my sister Sally howling? She is crying for both of us.

"Don't be scared!" my mother shouts to me. "If you fall out, try to reach a paddle or the edge of the canoe! I will help you!"

I can hardly hear her. Huge chunks of ice surround our canoe. They are crashing and smashing into each other, and making a terrible noise.

The canoe men are shouting orders to each other. They push the end of their paddles into each lump of ice, shoving it away from our canoe. They are trying to paddle us out of danger.

"If this goes on for another hour, we will pull our canoes out of the river, and wait for the ice to pass!" my father hollers.

We have stopped on the riverbank four times already, waiting for the ice to pass in front of us. Each time we go on the river again, the ice follows us. When the canoe spins sideways, my mother closes her eyes and grips my hand. She is going to have a baby soon, and I can see she is so tired. Sometimes I see her throwing up over the edge of the canoe.

My father has hired six strong men to take our family, and all of our belongings, to his home on the other side of the world. He wasted his money. We are definitely going to drown.

I knew we made a mistake when we left McLeod Lake. We thought the spring had come. We decided the river was safe for travel. The first group of voyageurs loaded all of their trading furs and pemmican into three canoes, and set out ahead of us. Then we packed our belongings in a fourth canoe—a big one—and climbed in.

My parents guessed we would reach Rocky Mountain Portage in just two days, because the current was strong. They didn't expect so much ice in the middle of May. We have been travelling on the river for six days, and I've been worried every minute.

I knew our trip would be hard. On the day before we left home, my father told me what to expect.

"We will travel five thousand miles to cross Rupert's Land and reach the place in the United States where I was born," he said. "You will go through the highest mountains you have ever seen, so high they poke their peaks through the clouds.

"Sometimes we will have to stop to carry our canoe on a portage around dangerous rocks. For days and days, you will ride in a canoe, walk on trails through the woods, and ride on carts over bumpy roads. It could be six months before we reach Vermont."

I didn't tell him that I already hate Vermont. I have a good reason.

Before I was born, my parents sent my brother George, who was only three years old, to live with Uncle Argalus in Vermont. My father told my mother that his first son needed to grow up in a land with schools and proper houses, not in a wild northern forest. She told me they cried together when they gave my brother to the people who would carry him into the canoe for his long journey to the east.

My brother waved goodbye with his chubby hand.

Little George arrived safely at my uncle's house, after many months of travel. He died later of a sudden sickness. He was only six years old.

Today I am eight years old, and healthy. I don't want to fall out of a canoe into the Peace River. I don't want to go to Vermont to get sick and die either.

My father says he wants to take his family out of this wilderness so we will have a better life. This is *my* wilderness. I like it just fine.

The river is quieter now, but I see big chunks of ice in the distance. I think we are still in danger. The big men are joking to each other in French as they paddle our canoes. Maybe I won't drown for a minute or two.

My father smokes his pipe and watches two eagles circle above our heads. In front of me, my mother whispers secrets to Sally. She speaks to us in the words of the Secwepemc people. My father speaks to us in Cree, the language of the fur trade. My parents talk to each other in French.

Are you confused yet? I know a few English words, but they stick on my tongue when I say them.

My father began to teach me to write English words on paper when I was six. I started with the English name he gave me. *Polly*.

"That's just your short name," he said. "Now I'll write your full name." He pushed the pen across the page, making curly letters. *Mary Patience Williams Harmon*.

It was a hot summer day, and we had been picking berries. My father taught me to write a juicy, delicious English word. *Strawberry*. That day I learned new words for the food in our garden. *Potato. Turnip. Barley.* My favourite English word is also my favourite food to eat—*salmon*—but the spelling is silly. Do you know how to say salmon in four languages? I do.

Oh no! Here comes more ice!

What do we know for sure?

The good news is that Polly Harmon didn't drown. The voyageurs paddled the canoe quickly to shore. The family waited until all the ice had passed before they continued their journey.

Polly's story begins in the place we now know as the Cariboo Country of northern British Columbia, west of the Rocky Mountains. Her father, Daniel Harmon, was a homesick American fur trader who worked for the North West Company. When Daniel was twenty-seven years old, he met a fourteen-year-old girl named Lizette Duval, the daughter of a Secwepemc mother from the Rockies and a French-Canadian fur trader. Lizette taught Daniel how to live in the northern country where she had been born. They lived together for the rest of their lives.

Polly was born at Stuart's Lake on May 8, 1811, the fourth of twelve children. Some of her brothers and sisters died when they were little.

We know about Polly's canoe trip through the ice, her English lessons on the summer day, and the sad story of her brother George, because her father kept an interesting diary. Daniel also explained in his diary about the way he and Lizette spoke different languages to their children at home.

As for the terrible trip on the Peace River, Polly and her family arrived safely at Rocky Mountain Portage on May 14, 1819. They travelled through the high Rockies into the territory we now call the Peace Country in northern Alberta. After crossing Rupert's Land—now western Canada—they stopped on August 18 at Fort William, a trading fort that is now the city of Thunder Bay, Ontario. Six days later, Polly's mother gave birth to a baby named John. She had no time to rest. The family still had a long way to go.

After their long, hard journey, Polly and her family arrived in Vermont in the United States in the late fall of 1819. They built a farm. In time, her parents had six more children, and the family moved back across the border to a home near Montreal. Polly's father, her younger sister, Sally, and another brother and sister died in a smallpox epidemic in 1843.

When Polly was nineteen, she married a machinist named Calvin Ladd. They raised eight children together. She died in Montreal in 1861 at the age of fifty.

Two boys and two bears

Keskayiwew, age fifteen, and younger brother Kôsihkosiwayâniw, near the Ghost Lakes, 1841

Tân'si! If you come hunting with us, you will need to be quiet.

You don't look like an experienced hunter. Can you shoot? Can you use a knife? Do you ever hunt in the woods to feed your little brothers and sisters?

Ssh! If you follow us, we don't want you to scare away the deer or the elk, or even the rabbits. Walk quietly. If you slap mosquitoes, and slash through the branches with your arms, every animal on both sides of the trail will hear you and run away.

We need to bring fresh meat to our family before it gets dark. My mother said she and the younger ones will wait for my father at the lake a little longer.

"He should be here soon," she said. "He promised to guide the boss of the fur traders to the headwaters of a big river. He wants us to go with them. He is bringing twenty men and forty-five horses to meet us here, and then we will ride together through the pass to the other side of the mountains."

I asked my mother why he was so late. "Where could he be?"

"I don't know where he is," she whispered. I could tell she didn't want the smaller ones to hear her. "He said he'd be here in early summer with fresh meat from the hunters and winter trade goods from Fort Edmonton. It is almost the end of August. He knows we have to leave here before winter."

I began to worry that my father had crossed the trail of a Pikani war party. Was he in trouble? Did he need me?

My mother's worried eyes told me she needed me more. She and her sisters have a big family to feed, and babies to carry, and I'm old enough to hunt larger game away from our camp.

I left the camp early this morning with my younger brother. My mother gave us a small bag of pemmican and some bannock, and asked us to come back soon. I carried my father's old rifle with some bullets.

"We won't be back until we can bring some food," I told her.

All morning we walked along a creek, following the soft footprints of a mule deer, as it led us along a muddy shore. Somewhere we lost the deer tracks. We stopped to snare and skin a small *wâpos* for our meal. Our mouths watered as we roasted the rabbit meat over a small campfire. It smelled so good, and it was almost ready to eat.

Suddenly, I heard a small, swishing sound in the bush behind me.

"I think our little sister has followed us here," I whispered to Kôsihkosiwayâniw." He looked into the bush and nodded.

I waited for a small girl's voice to say: "Keskayiwew, can you give me some of that tasty rabbit?"

To our surprise, a hungry visitor stumbled into our camp, and it wasn't my sister.

A small bear cub raced towards Kôsihkosiwayâniw, snorting and sniffing in the air for a feast.

My brother was startled. He ran around the little bear. He still thought my little sister was hiding behind a spruce tree, and he wanted to protect her. Of course, she had never been there at all. The cub had made the noise we heard.

I am not frightened of *maskwa*—I respect them—but I know how they behave. When I saw the little bear, I knew a *nâpemaskwa*, a mother bear, would be somewhere close by. She would be angry that my brother was standing between her and her cub. Growling and grumpy, she would arrive soon in a bad temper.

"Go up the tree!" I shouted to my brother.

He scooted up the nearest tall tree in a few seconds. As I expected, I soon heard the crashing, smashing sound of an angry mother bear heading towards our campfire.

I didn't waste a moment to grab the old rifle on the ground. As fast as my feet would move, I climbed another tall tree.

"Keep climbing," I shouted to my brother. "Bears can climb too!"

We climbed as far up as we could, and tried to keep perfectly still above the spruce branches. A cold wind pushed each tree back and forth. With every gust, I thought I would tumble into the jaws of a hungry bear.

I heard the branch below me creak, crack . . . and break! I quickly reached for another branch, and swung my legs over it to pull myself to a higher hiding place.

Down below, the mother bear raced toward her cub on all four legs. When she reached him, she cuffed him on the back of the ear with one paw. I could hear her growling and snorting at the bottom of my quivering, shivering tree. She was sniffing the air. Would that be me she was after?

I looked across the treetops to my brother's worried face.

"Will she come after us?" he whispered hoarsely from his branch. I shook my head. The truth was that I didn't know.

We watched and waited.

With one paw, the little cub scooped saskatoon berries into his open mouth. He was as hungry as us.

The mother bear stood up to her full, terrifying height. She opened her giant jaws to reveal huge, sharp biting teeth. With one swoop of her paw, she grabbed our roast rabbit from the campfire, stuffed it into her mouth, and swallowed it in one big gulp.

Then she turned around and trudged off into the forest, with her cub scrambling after her. They left us alone.

We waited for a little while, just to be sure, then we jumped down from our trees.

Now we are tracking a deer into a canyon. We will follow the mountain trail, hoping to meet our father as he makes his way home to us. Will you help us with the hunt?

What do we know for sure?

We don't know whether Keskayiwew and Kôsihkosiwayâniw encountered a bear and her cub while hunting in the Rockies as young boys. This part of the story is imaginary.

We do know a lot about the boys and their family.

The boys' father was Pesew, the head chief of the Mountain Cree. He was also known in the French language as Louis Piché. He was an experienced guide who led many fur traders and travellers through the Rockies and as far south as the Missouri River, from the 1820s until his death in 1845.

His family usually travelled across the mountains and plains with him, but they always returned to their hunting territory and camp in the mountains near the lake we now know as Lake Minnewanka in Banff National Park.

The boys' mother was Opitaskewis. In August of 1841, she waited with her family near the Ghost Lakes for Pesew to join her.

Pesew was late, as the story says. Sir George Simpson, the governor of the Hudson's Bay Company, had hired the Cree chief to guide him for his first long journey from Fort Edmonton, across the Rockies to the headwaters of the Columbia River.

With Pesew leading the way, twenty-two men and forty-five horses travelled into the mountains between the Ghost River and Devil's Gap, and made their way to the long, open valley toward the chain of Ghost Lakes. Simpson named the last lake after his guide—he called him Peechee in English, perhaps his own way of saying Piché. While the federal government changed the name of Lake Peechee to Lake Minnewanka in 1888, you can still see Mount Peechee in Banff, named after the Cree leader and mountain guide.

When Pesew and Simpson arrived at the meeting place beside the lake, they found nobody there. Simpson wrote, "Madam Peechee and the children had left their encampment, probably on account of a scarcity of game." The men continued their journey through the mountains, and Pesew's family was reunited later.

The two boys would have spoken Cree all the time, far more than the few words of Cree in this story. The Cree word *tân'si* means hello. *Maskwa* means bear, *nâpemaskwa* means mother bear, and *wâpos* means rabbit.

The two boys grew up to be important Cree chiefs, famous in the history of Alberta.

Born in 1826, the older brother Keskayiwew would have been fifteen at the time of this story. He was known in French as Alexis Piché, and in English as Bobtail. His younger brother, Kôsihkosiwayâniw, was known as Jean-Baptiste Piché in French, and Ermineskin in English.

Keskayiwew signed an adhesion, or addition, to Treaty 6 in 1877. Their large families claimed a reserve in the Bear Hills —*Maskwachees*—which sparked the idea for this story. That is the reserve that we now call Hobbema, south of Edmonton.

Keskayiwew later withdrew from the treaty, because he said Canada had broken its treaty promises. He took his family and many others south to Montana. He returned, however, and died in 1900; his younger brother died a few years later.

Many of their descendants live on the large reserve at Hobbema, and across Canada and the US.

One of Keskayiwew's great-grandsons, Chief Robert Smallboy, led members of his band—including many children—away from Hobbema, and back to the foothills of the Rockies in 1964. A recipient of the Order of Canada, Smallboy died in 1984. Smallboy's Camp continues to exist as a community in the foothills south of Hinton, and many Cree kids have grown up there.

The runaway girl

Betsy Fraser, age twelve,
Jasper House and Lake of Islands, 1845

Sit down beside the fire. I didn't notice you here before. I thought I had counted everybody: my parents, my four sisters, my little brother, the laughing priest from America, the family of Louis L'Iroquois, some Berlands, some Desjarlais and Chalifoux—altogether fifty-four people and twenty dogs in one camp.

I guess I missed you. How did you find your way here?

We came to this lake for a funny reason. My parents lost their patience with our visitors. Here's how it happened.

A month ago, a priest travelled into our territory on horseback. His name is Father De Smet. He visited the Carrier band and the Iroquois voyageurs, and then he came to our trading post at Jasper House. Many people followed him to our place, because we haven't seen a priest in these mountains for seven years.

"Will you marry us, please?" many couples said. The priest married people all day and half the night.

"Will you put holy water on the heads of our children?" some parents said. The priest baptized forty-four people and wrote down each name.

Lots of people arrived at Jasper House just to listen to the adventure stories of this stranger who had travelled all the way from St. Louis on the Mississippi to our fur-trading post in the northern mountains.

On the morning of the fifteenth day, my mother grabbed my father by the arm and said: "Colin, we are running out of food. The priest likes to eat! How will we feed all these people?"

"We won't!" my father replied, with a thump of his walking stick. "I have a better idea."

The next morning, my father told all the men, women, and children—and the priest too—that we would walk together to the Lake of Islands to make a big camp. "The best hunters can go hunting, and the rest of us can fish," he said. "We will eat plenty and have a good time together."

I could tell that Father De Smet liked that idea. He is a large, round man who loves nothing better than a good pheasant stew.

We walked to the lake and set up our tipis among the lodgepole pines.

The priest doesn't seem to notice all the kids and dogs running around the camp. He sits on a rock, looks up at the mountains, and writes in a small book. Each time the hunters return, he writes down a list of everything they bring us to eat. He likes to read his list out loud. Twelve moose deer, two reindeer, thirty large mountain sheep, two porcupines, two hundred and ten hares, one beaver, two muskrats, twenty-four buzzards, one hundred and fifteen ducks, twenty-one pheasants, one snipe, one eagle, one owl.

The priest counts the fish the men catch too. They bring us between thirty and fifty whitefish and twenty trout every day.

What a feast we have every night! We don't like to boast, of course.

"Our living is hard around here," we tell the priest. "Our country is poor. Our stomachs are often empty."

Father De Smet looks at us with questions in his eyes. His bushy eyebrows go up and down. I think he knows we are joking.

My father plays the bagpipes for him. My mother stirs sugar into the hot tea in his tin cup. Whenever she lifts the stew pot from the fire, the priest looks happier and happier. After we finish eating, and we are so full we can't eat another crumb of bannock, old Louis L'Iroquois and the other visitors tell stories as the moon rises over the mountains.

That's how I heard the story about the runaway girl. Would you like to hear it? I think this story might be true.

About three years before I was born, a small band of the Snaring people camped on a point of land near the fur-trading post called Jasper House.

The Assiniboine people considered these people their enemies, because they came from the other side of the mountains. One day, they invited the Snaring men to their camp, saying they wanted to talk about peace. It was a trick. A battle followed, and when it was over, most of the Snaring people had been killed. Of the thirty-seven people in their camp, only ten people escaped into the woods.

The Assiniboine captured three Snaring girls— each one about seventeen years old—and took them along on their journey to Fort Assiniboine. A Métis trader named Mr. Bellerose heard that three young women were tied up in a tipi. Late at night, he sneaked into the tipi, cut the ropes around their wrists, and set them free.

"Here, take this," he said. He gave them a small fire bag containing everything they needed to start a campfire, and a knife. Then he had to hurry away in case he was caught.

The girls ran into the woods and made their way into the mountains. They had an argument when they reached the mouth of the Berland River. Two girls took the fire bag, and followed the Athabasca River. They were never heard of again.

The last girl took the knife, and followed the Berland River by herself for about thirty miles. Falling leaves swirled around her, and the nights were very cold. She gathered wood and somehow made herself a small shelter for the winter. She lived on berries and squirrels, at first, but she made small traps and caught rabbits for food. She made clothes of rabbit skins, and also caught porcupines and marmots and other small animals.

When summer came, she walked into the territory of the Iroquois, who had come west from Montreal as voyageurs. An Iroquois hunter from Grande Cache found her footprints in the mud, but he was frightened that she was a weetigo—a person with a bad spirit—and he didn't follow the tracks.

The girl worked hard that summer to hunt small animals and dry the meat for the long winter. At this time it was very cold in the mountains and foothills, with howling winds and deep snow, but she knew how to feed herself.

The second summer came. The Iroquois hunter returned to the same place in the woods, and saw a woman's footprints again. This time, he followed them. He noticed small animal traps and places where bark had been stripped from the trees, and soon he reached a cave in the side of a hill. Nearby he found a neat stack of wood and a small campfire.

Hiding in the woods with his gun ready, he waited. He was a bit scared. Soon the girl approached her campfire with more wood. Looking at her, the Iroquois hunter realized that she must be one of the three lost girls of the Snaring band.

Suddenly, she looked up. As soon as she caught sight of the hunter—the first person she had seen in two years—she was terrified. She tried to run away, and struggled when the Iroquois hunter finally caught up to her.

"Don't worry, I will take you home to live with my family," he said, but she didn't trust him. He had a lot of trouble bringing her back to his camp, but when she saw his family, she became calmer.

The runaway girl lived with the hunter's family for two years. Then she worked at Jasper House for another two years as a servant to a trader's wife. One day a Snaring band brought furs to trade at the trading post, and she recognized them as her relatives. She rode away with them, and they say she is still alive, with a family of her own.

—

"Could this story be true?" I asked my mother at the campfire. She was too busy cooking to hear my question.

Father De Smet made everyone laugh when he said he had to leave our camp in order to stop eating. The traders at Fort Edmonton told him he would need to eat less food or he would be too slow and heavy to make his way on snowshoes over the mountains to Fort Vancouver.

We stood beside the lake to say goodbye to him. All the men pointed their guns to the top of the highest mountain, and shot a salute to honour the visitor. "We will name that mountain after you," said Louis L'Iroquois. Then we shouted three cheers, and the priest waved goodbye.

Are you going to stay here? We could pretend we were the runaway girls, and find a cave for a shelter. Let's run away right now!

—

What do we know for sure?

Betsy Fraser, the girl who told this story, was born on June 28, 1833, at Fort Edmonton in Rupert's Land. She was the oldest daughter of a Scottish-born fur trader, Colin Fraser, and his French-speaking Cree Métis wife, Nancy Beaudry.

Betsy rode on horseback to Jasper House with her parents

when she was two years old. Her family lived at this small trading post in the mountains for the next fifteen years.

Jasper House looked like a small cabin, made of rough logs. The family lived in one small room. In the other room, hunters and trappers brought furs to trade for blankets, hunting guns, pots and beads, and other things they needed.

The Fraser family had twelve children as the years went by, and many visitors, so Jasper House must have been crowded most of the time.

Pierre-Jean De Smet, a Catholic missonary, visited the trading post in 1845, when Betsy was twelve years old. Many people came to Jasper House to see the priest, including the old Iroquois voyageur Louis Kwarakwante, also known as Louis L'Iroquois, Louis Calliheue, or the Sun Traveller, and his thirty-six family members. Everyone decided to make a camp together at a place called the Lake of Islands so they could hunt for more food and catch fish.

The priest described everything that happened at the camp in his notes and letters. He described the way his friends had named a mountain after him, shooting a salute to say goodbye. The priest also joked that he ate too much, and that he was too big to travel on horseback in the mountains. A year later, he published an interesting book, *Oregon Missions and Travels Over the Rocky Mountains*, about his adventures. You can see Roche De Smet today as you drive through Jasper National Park. The community of Callihoo, near Spruce Grove, Alberta, is named after the descendants of Louis L'Iroquois.

And what about the story of the runaway girl? Did she really live alone in the mountains for two years?

We will never know for sure, but many people have told this story over the years.

Father De Smet wrote that he met the young woman with her people just after he left Jasper House and the big camp. Many years later, a fur trader named Henry John Moberly said he met the woman with her family at Tête Jaune Cache, a trading place in the mountains in what is now British Columbia. The priest and the fur trader told the same story in the same way—so the details could be true.

If you go to Jasper National Park today, you might camp at the Snaring River campground. The river is named after the girl's relatives, who were killed. We don't know which lake in the national park is the one that Betsy and her family called Lake of the Islands.

When Betsy Fraser grew up, she married William Borwick, who was a blacksmith at Fort Edmonton. She gave birth to nine babies, but at least three died in childhood.

Thousands of kids who live in Alberta today can trace their family roots to the people in this story.

A Métis family in a Red River cart.

Colin's courage

Colin Sinclair, age nine,
Upper Kananaskis Pass, 1854

I am too tired to take another step. Can you help me? Can you take this rope, and lead the oxen for awhile?

I have been walking through snow up to my waist all morning. My fingers are icicles. I can't push my feet forward anymore. If I slip on these boulders again, I don't think I will be able to get up.

I want to pull a buffalo robe over my shoulders and close my eyes for a minute of forgetting. I am aching to sleep.

Please, don't let me lie down in the snow. Talk to me to keep me awake.

Do you have any food to share? I had a few sips of pemmican soup this morning, but I gave my bannock to my sisters. My step-mother says we are almost out of pemmican, flour, and tea.

"We thought the hunters would find wild game easily, but they came back yesterday with nothing," she said. "Maybe we are too high on the mountain now, and the animals are in the forest down below."

We can't eat rock or snow or clouds, and that's all we see up here. I yank and pull the stubborn oxen over the slippery trail. I daydream about a venison feast. I can almost smell the roast meat, sizzling over the fire, but I know my mind is playing a cruel trick on me.

We are so hungry. Each family is measuring food so that we

will be able eat a bit each morning. We need strength to climb. Even our oxen are slowing down. Maybe their stomachs are grumbling too. My baby sister, Lucy Agnes, is crying on my mother's back. I can see ice crystals sticking to her brown eyelashes.

Maybe we should never have started this trip. I remember Mrs. Bird's warning. A few days after we left home, we stopped at White Horse Plain. The sun suddenly disappeared from the sky. For a few minutes, night was stuck in the middle of day.

"Our journey will go wrong," Mrs. Bird said, covering her eyes with her shawl. "Trouble will follow us over the mountains to Oregon."

I laughed at her that day. Superstitious old lady. My father told everyone we had witnessed a natural event, a total eclipse of the sun, and bad luck had nothing to do with it. I believed him.

Now I'm not so sure.

At the start, I thought this would be an easy summer adventure. Snaring rabbits. Racing ponies. Maybe a buffalo hunt on the plains if we were lucky. I was travelling with my family and my friends on an exciting journey to the new Oregon territory. I thought we could laugh our way from our home in Red River to the Pacific Ocean.

My father is leading one hundred people to settle in Oregon—twenty-eight grown-up men, eleven grown-up women, and sixty-one kids of different ages. There are a few babies, lots of children like me, and some older brothers and sisters too young to marry yet.

We set off from home in a long, long line of rumbling ox carts.

Our parade of families was one mile long if you measured it. Aunt Meg drove our cart, because my mother was too busy with the babies to struggle with a dumb ox.

We moved steadily west in a cloud of prairie dust, the wooden wheels creaking and shrieking from morning until night.

My father and the other men rode beside us on horseback, herding our cattle and moving them forward. Stubborn Mr. Sutherland tried hard to keep track of his three hundred sheep, which he had insisted on bringing, even though my father frowned at him.

We camped on the plains every night. My father hollered the same words at dawn for months. "Every man to his ox!" This was his signal to everyone, not just the men. We would hurry around camp, bringing in the cattle, harnessing oxen to carts, tying the buffalo robes in place, scooping up the little kids who struggled to get away.

Each family took its place in the line of carts. We waited for my father's arm signal. "Move out!"

Our oxen are slow, grumpy, stubborn, and not too smart. Sometimes we travelled only two and a half miles in an hour. We left Red River in early May and didn't reach Fort Edmonton until the end of July.

Our disasters started early in the trip. And I'm not just talking about nasty mosquitoes and bulldog flies.

At the Qu'Appelle River, my Uncle John was leading our cart down the steep riverbank in the pouring rain, holding on to my shirt so I wouldn't fall into the water, and he slipped in the mud. The cart wheels ran right over him and hurt his back, but the accident didn't kill him.

Floods on the Saskatchewan River blocked our way twice. We knew that we couldn't cross the high river in our carts without drowning. We had to pull the wagon wheels from our carts, and pile everything on rafts, to float our belongings across the dangerous water. The frightened animals had to swim across.

We arrived at Fort Pitt to hear a noise I will never forget—the scary barking of almost three hundred sled dogs outside the log walls. On that awful night, the dogs attacked and killed all of Mr. Sutherland's sheep. Mrs. Brown gave birth to her baby boy in the middle all of the barking and bleeting and shouting.

We were lucky to meet Maskepetoon and his band on our way to Fort Edmonton. The Cree chief was an old friend of my father's.

"I will guide your families through a new pass over the mountains," he promised us. "This one is shorter than the one we took last time."

We needed Maskepetoon's help. His family gave us food, and helped us to build eight bridges over flooded rivers so that we could reach Fort Edmonton without trouble.

All day I watched for smoke on the horizon. I jumped at every strange sound in the night. I was nervous for a reason.

The Cree and the Blackfoot are at war. We are travelling with the Cree people, who are our relations. The Blackfoot people don't want us near them in a summer of battles.

The people at Fort Edmonton locked their gates when they saw a cloud of dust on the horizon. They didn't know the cloud was us. We waved a white flag to show them we were their friends.

The gates swung open. Inside the old trading post, my father warned us about difficult times ahead for us in the mountains.

"We might have to leave our oxen behind and climb the trails by pack horse, so we have work to do," he said. "I want you to make new saddles. Buy new horses. Find warmer clothing, more blankets, and buffalo robes. Store more hunting guns. Pack more pemmican."

For one month, we prepared for the hardest part of our journey. Maskepetoon led us south and west into the mountains. One night as we camped in the Bow River Valley, a Blackfoot raiding party of forty men killed seven cattle and stole three horses, but the warriors didn't hurt us.

Then Mrs. Flett had her baby in our night camp beside the river. The baby died a few days later. We had to stop for fifteen days until the sad woman was feeling well enough to travel into the mountains.

When my father told everyone to smash up their Red River carts, and leave them behind, many people became angry with him.

"We can't do that!" they said. "Without the carts we will have no shelter at night. We don't have enough pack horses to carry all our belongings over the mountains!"

My father tried to explain that our wide carts would tumble into the canyons from the narrow trails at the top of the mountains.

"We will use all our pack horses and most oxen to carry our food and equipment," he said. "Only women with babies will ride on oxen or horses. They will put the infants on their backs, and hold the smallest children in their arms. Older girls and boys, and all men, will walk."

A Métis family, leaving the camp.

So we began to walk into the mountains, climbing for hours and hours. Each day became harder. Our fathers slashed a narrow path through the trees and underbrush with their axes. Our mothers and the older kids pushed and pulled oxen and horses over rocks and boulders, over fallen trees, through swamps and rapids.

I guessed that we were lost, but my parents would not answer my questions about that. We climbed on a twisting path up the mountain. I walked between a steep cliff on one side and a deep canyon on the other. If I took one wrong step, I knew I could fall to my death.

We came to a canyon high above rushing, smashing rapids. The men built a log bridge strong enough for horses, oxen, and people to cross to the other side. With each footstep, I held my breath.

"Don't look down," my stepmother whispered. "Four more steps."

I made it across, but I was trembling like a sparrow in winter.

We ran out of food a few days later. We had to kill some of our oxen for meat. That meant each person had to carry supplies, even the children. The mountain trail became too steep, and too dangerous for any horse or oxen to take a rider.

My father looked at everyone with pity in his eyes.

"I'm sorry, but we will all have to walk now. If you have the strength, please carry an infant or a small child."

I carried Jenny for as long as I could. She is only two years old, but heavy. When the blizzard began, my big brother, Henry, took my sister from my arms.

"You need all of your strength to push through the snow," he said. "Walk behind me, and watch my shoulders, and don't stop for anything."

I am walking through snow up to my armpits. I am too cold to cry. Will I live through this day?

What do we know for sure?

Colin Sinclair did survive his worst day in the Kananaskis Pass in October 1854. We know that because John Campbell, one of the men on the trip, described the travellers' courage that day as they stumbled through heavy snowdrifts, a metre deep, over the summit of the Rockies.

All of the events described in the story—from the sun's eclipse to Colin's troubles in the mountains—are taken from the travellers' accounts of the difficult trip.

Born in 1845, Colin Sinclair was nine years old when he travelled across the continent and over the mountains.

Young Colin belonged to a well-known Métis family in the Red River settlement, an early community near present-day Winnipeg, Manitoba. The Métis people—who could trace their family roots to both First Nations and European ancestors—considered Red River an important gathering place in their huge western territory.

Colin's father, James Sinclair, was an experienced Métis fur trader, and also an agent for the Hudson's Bay Company and the British government, although his family didn't know it. He took two groups of Red River settlers, mostly Métis families, to the Pacific coast to try to establish a British settlement there before too many American settlers arrived. The plan didn't work. The area soon became part of the United States, but descendants of these Métis Canadian settlers still live in Oregon.

As a boy, Colin spoke Cree, English, and French, the languages of the Red River Métis. His mother, Elizabeth Bird Sinclair, died when he was a small baby, after giving birth to nine children. Three years later, his father married another woman, Mary Campbell, and they had three more children. Colin's grandmother, Nahovway, was Cree and also lived at Red River. Some of his brothers and sisters died when he was young.

On the trip across the Rockies in 1854, Colin travelled with his father and stepmother, Mary; his aunt Meg; his older sister, Maria, who was nineteen; his brother, Henry, who was sixteen;

and two little sisters, Jennie Jane, a one-year-old, and Agnes Lucy, a newborn baby. His adventures continued after he left the mountains. The Red River settlers rode south toward the Pacific Ocean on easy trails, but the territory was more dangerous because some local tribes did not welcome newcomers.

Seven months after they left Red River, Colin and his family arrived safely at Fort Walla Walla on December 16, 1854. Sadly, the boy's father, James Sinclair, was killed four months later, when the Cascade tribe attacked a small store that he was visiting in the middle of a battle.

Colin and his brother and sisters were waiting nearby in a safer place when their father was killed. Their stepmother had no money, land, or cattle. Life was difficult for the family for many years, but finally, Ulysses S. Grant, an old friend of James Sinclair, became the president of the United States. Colin's stepmother appealed to him for help, and he arranged a special Act of Congress to give the family 640 acres of land in the Walla Walla Valley, in present-day Oregon.

We know from Métis genealogical records that young Colin grew up, and at the age of forty-eight, he married Mary Rowena Philipps. The couple had nine children. Colin died in British Columbia at the age of sixty-five on June 20, 1910.

Despite the hardships they endured, the story of the brave settlers who travelled across the western part of the continent from Red River to Oregon in 1841 and 1854 is barely remembered in Canada. On both trips, there were dozens of children under the age of sixteen, including many toddlers and infants, and several babies born on the way. Maybe the youngest ones were the bravest of all.

Skunk stew

Augustus Schubert, Jr., age five,
Cow Dung Lake, 1862

Go away! You can't push that stew into my mouth. My lips are shut tight. My teeth are a wall against your spoon.

Your stupid skunk stew smells like sickening skunk stink.

I will not open my mouth. I will not let that stew touch my tongue. If you make me sip a spoonful, I will spit it out on your apron. I will spew that stew all over your old wool stockings.

I am warning you, Mama.

Don't tell me you put a little salt in this stew, or tasty bits of ox tail, or roast grouse, or chunks of pemmican, or a potato, or a sweet onion you saved all the way from our kitchen in Red River. That's a lie. I have heard your stories before.

I know our good food is all gone. You gave us the last dry scraps in the saddlebag four days ago.

Don't lie to me again. I am five. I am smart.

When you told me that it was buffalo stew, I knew it was porcupine fat, fried in a pan until it was a grey mush.

When you told me that it was roast duck soup, I knew it was dry crow bones, thrown in a pot of muddy river water.

I watched you at the campfire yesterday. I heard the big man from Ontario say: "I am so hungry I could eat a skunk from the back-end forward." I looked at you, stared right into your eyes, and I saw you stand up and walk into the woods.

Later I saw you holding your nose as you stirred the glop in the iron pot. Keep away from me with that mess of stink on your spoon. I know what you will say: "Eat it, Gus, I know your stomach is empty. You will feel full if you eat this good stew. You will sleep better, too. I am worried about you. My little boy, you are too thin."

I don't care if I'm as skinny as a nail, as or as bent as a horseshoe.

I won't eat skunk hot. I won't eat skunk cold.

I won't eat skunk soup, roast skunk, skunk dumplings, sliced skunk, and no matter what you tell me, I won't eat skunk stew.

Take your spoonful of smell to Mary Jane or to James. They might swallow your story about the delicious morsel of roast goose that you cooked just for them.

I am stronger than my little sister and brother. I have been hungry for three days, and I haven't cried once.

My stomach grumbles all day. When I fall asleep at night, I dream about soft, warm bread until I can taste the melting butter on my lips, and feel it dribbling down my chin. As soon as I close my eyes, I dip Irish oat cakes into milky tea. I taste sweet honey on my tongue.

When I wake up in the morning, my mouth is dry and my lips are cracked. I lie on the frozen spruce boughs, shivering and cold as ice. I know the feeling of empty. I feel like I have a hard stone in my belly.

You are my mother. You can make me walk through dark, scary woods. You can make me ride on a broken raft over rapids.

You can make me climb a mountain trail, up and up and up, and when it gets dark, you can say: "Just one more hour, Gus. Keep climbing one more hour and we'll stop to make our night camp."

You can make me climb for two more hours, through a thunderstorm, with the icy rain and wind in my face, and the coyotes howling from the cliffs above my head.

You can promise me all the gold in the Cariboo if I just taste the slop on your wooden spoon. I don't want your gold. I won't eat your slippery, slimy, stinking skunk stew!

What do we know for sure?

Augustus Schubert, Jr., age five, travelled with 137 people—mostly grown-up men—on a difficult trip across the West in 1862.

His family was trying to reach the gold rush territory of the Cariboo Country in the wilderness of British Columbia.

Little Gus was born two days before Christmas in 1856, near the Mississippi River in the territory that became Minnesota. His father, Augustus, came from Germany. His mother, Catherine, came from Ireland. They sold beer and whisky to men in a tavern inside the log cabin where Gus was born.

The family had two more babies—Mary Jane and James—and then ran into a lot of bad luck. They moved to the Red River settlement—in what later became Manitoba—and joined a big group of travellers as they headed west across the prairies in horse-drawn wagons.

Gus's mother was expecting another baby, but she kept that a secret so that the other gold prospectors would accept the Schubert family on the trip.

The travellers called themselves the Overlanders. After resting

50

in Fort Edmonton, they travelled across the Rocky Mountains, through the Yellowhead Pass, then known as Tête Jaune's Pass.

This part of the trip brought one disaster after another. The Overlanders walked hundreds of kilometres, and got lost many times in the thick forest. They fell into rivers, and some men drowned. They lost horses. In the mountains, the travellers had to eat some of their last oxen. They weren't always good hunters. As they travelled through the Rockies, they ran out of food and couldn't find more.

According to the diaries and letters of the travellers, they did eat skunk, porcupine, and crow at a camp near Cow Dung Lake, now known for good reason as Yellowhead Lake.

We don't know for sure if little Gus made a fuss over skunk stew. We do know that many five-year-olds are known to be stubborn at meal times. One Cariboo gold prospector later said that an Ontario man had muttered: "I am so hungry I could eat a skunk from the back-end forward." Those words were the spark for this story.

In Kamloops, at the end of his family's terrible five-month journey, and after a final hike that lasted for many days, Gus's mother gave birth to a baby girl named Rosa. Many people think Catherine was the only woman on the trip, but that's not true. Three Métis women, and their children, completed the journey with the Schubert family.

Little Gus, the five-year-old, did not suffer poor health after his trip. He grew up with his family in the Spallumcheen Valley of British Columbia, married, and became a farmer near Cache Creek. He died in 1946 at the age of ninety-nine.

Rocky Mountain travellers: (left to right) Louis Battenotte's
thirteen-year-old son, Lord Milton, Dr. Walter Cheadle, the Nakoda guide
Louis Battenotte, and his unidentified wife, at their camp in 1863.

AS SEEN IN CHEADLE'S JOURNAL OF TRIP ACROSS
CANADA, 1862–1863, BY WALTER B. CHEADLE

Help! I'm stuck with Old Belly Ache!

Louis Battenotte's son, age thirteen,
Tête Jaune's Trail, 1863

Do you know how to cut down trees to build a raft? Can you ride a bucking horse across a wild river? If the rapids pull the horse into deep water, can you rescue him?

Can you fish for trout, or hunt for mountain sheep, or build a shelter in a thunderstorm?

If you come along with me, I can promise you plenty of fun and adventure, but I need help in a hurry. I am travelling through the mountains with three strangers who couldn't find their way across a field of grass by themselves.

The three strangers—Rich Man, Strong Man, and Belly Ache—asked my parents to guide them from Fort Edmonton to Jasper House, and through the Rocky Mountains to the other side.

"We will pay you three English pounds a month," Rich Man promised my father. "If you stay with us until the end of the trip, we will pay you an extra five pounds."

My father looked at each man carefully. He looked at Belly Ache's soft hands and skinny feet, and he whispered to me and to my mother in our language: "My friends warned me about this man. I need you both to come with us. These men don't know our territory. This lazy one will be useless in the mountain country."

The baby in our family had just died, and we needed to travel to get away from our sad feelings. We loaded our pack horses and left Fort Edmonton at the beginning of the summer. My dog came too. By the time we reached Colin Fraser's house at Lac Ste. Anne, we knew the three strangers would bring trouble to us.

They fight too much. They don't hit each other with their fists, or pull knives or guns, but they yell at each other all day and half the night.

Rich Man loses his temper every minute. He is sick a lot of the time, holding his head and falling down, so he brought Strong Man to give him medicine.

Belly Ache complains all day. He is the laziest man I have ever met, and the noisiest. He refuses to learn my name, and he thinks I am on this earth to serve him.

"My feet hurt, Boy!" he says to me. "Pack my horse!"

I call him Belly Ache because he is always moaning and groaning about something. He has a long face like a horse, a big nose like a hawk's beak, and no teeth. He wears a long, woolly coat, a tall, black hat, and flapping pants. Strings hold up his narrow, little boots.

One night on the trail, Belly Ache sat down to rest with his boots off. A confused horse ran through the campfire, and dragged sparks and hot ashes into the woods. Soon a big forest fire started! We grabbed axes and started chopping down trees, and fetching water, to save ourselves.

Belly Ache just sat on the ground, looking at his toes.

"Why the devil don't you bring some water!" Strong Man yelled at him.

"I ca-a-a-n't," moaned Belly Ache. "I've only got one boot on."

We soon learned that Belly Ache could not ride a horse very

well. Once we found him sitting on a log, crying, because he was so frightened of bears.

"Slow down!" he cries to us on the trail. "If you don't wait for me, the grizzly bears will surely devour me!"

My mother says she wishes the bears would do us a favour. Our friend Baptiste Supernat rode with us from Fort Edmonton, but he was so disgusted with our companions that he turned around and left us at the McLeod River. One day my father decided to teach Belly Ache a lesson. He quietly circled behind him in the woods, and growled like a bear.

Belly Ache screeched and hurried ahead for a few minutes, but soon he started to whine and slow down again. That night, at the campfire, I had another idea. I pulled a buffalo robe over my shoulders, and crawled on my hands and knees through the willows nearby.

"Grr!"

"Eek, what was that? A bear? "

"Grr!"

"There it is! I see it! I will expire! We are doomed!"

I stood up and bowed. The joke made me feel better.

Our journey was nothing to joke about. When we reached Roche Miette, we found the river in a flood. We couldn't cross it. We had to convince our hard-working horses to carry their heavy loads up the steep, twisting trail to the top of the ridge at Disaster Point.

You can imagine what Belly Ache thought of that. "Oh, mercy me, I will die on my knees on this mountain," he cried out. "I cannot go on!"

The boy pulls the horse up the mountain near Jasper House, 1863.
AS SEEN IN CHEADLE'S JOURNAL OF TRIP ACROSS
CANADA, 1862–1863, BY WALTER B. CHEADLE

He left his horse at the bottom of the hill, and huffed and puffed to the top of the ridge on his two flat feet, grumbling all the way. I had to rescue his poor horse for him, and climb the ridge myself for the second time.

We rode into the valley between the mountains, looking up at the snowy peaks in the sunlight. When we reached the Athabasca River, we found that it was also flooded, and too dangerous for us to cross.

"We'll stop here," my father said. We knew we would have to make a raft to cross the river safely with so many heavy packs.

All day, in the summer heat, with mosquitoes nibbling our necks and ears, we chopped down trees and carried logs to the river.

My father and the Strong Man carried the heaviest logs together. My mother and I carried heavy logs too, one of us on each end.

Can you guess what Belly Ache did?

He sat behind the bushes, smoked his pipe, and read a book. When Rich Man insisted that he help us, Belly Ache picked up one end of the lightest log. He started to complain right away.

"Oh dear, oh dear," he cried. "This is most painful. It is cutting my shoulder in two. Not so fast, my lord! Gently, gently. Steady, my lord, steady! I must stop! I shall drop with exhaustion directly! Oh!"

Suddenly, Belly Ache dropped his end of the log. Rich Man fell forward and hurt his shoulder. Belly Ache didn't notice. "Look what happened!" he moaned. "I have a scratch on my finger."

My mother warned us that this man might be the death of us. "The hardest part of this trip is ahead of us," she said. "These men don't understand the dangers ahead." My parents have been talking about leaving the three men at Jasper House, and going back to Fort Edmonton. The trouble is that they like Strong Man. He is a good rider and hunter, and he is learning our language. He is becoming our friend.

"I'll take care of the troublemaker from now on," Strong Man told us. "Please guide us through the mountains. We'll get lost without your help."

Today we had to cross a deep, rushing river. Belly Ache hates his horse, so he jumped off and tried to walk through the rapids, holding his walking stick. He fell into a deep hole with a splash, and spit water in all directions.

"Oh dear! Oh dear! I shall be carried off!"

Crossing a river in the mountains.
AS SEEN IN CHEADLE'S JOURNAL OF TRIP ACROSS
CANADA, 1862–1863, BY WALTER B. CHEADLE

Rich Man rode his horse into the rapids to rescue him. Belly Ache grabbed the stirrup, and floated to shore on his belly. Do you think he thanked anyone?

"Boy, take my wet trousers!" he ordered. "Spread them out to dry on the bushes!"

Can you see why I need your help? Can you meet us at Tête Jaune Cache? I'll be watching for you.

What do we know for sure?

We know that a thirteen-year old boy helped his parents guide three travellers through the Rockies in 1863.

We don't know his first name, because nobody wrote it down. The boy's father was Louis Battenotte, a hunter and guide who had been raised by the Nakoda people.

The three travellers called Louis Battenotte "The Assiniboine," because that's what English-speaking people called the Nakoda people at that time.

They called the son "The Boy" or "The Young One," and they called his mother "Mrs. Assiniboine."

All of the details in the story—including the time when the boy pretended to be a bear—come from Dr. Walter Cheadle's travel diary or the adventure book he wrote later with Lord Milton.

I imagined that the boy might have made up his own nicknames for the three men.

The Rich Man was William Wentworth-Fitzwilliam—Lord Milton, for short—a twenty-three-year-old English gentleman who had many serious health problems, and a bad temper.

The Strong Man was Dr. Cheadle, a good horseman and a twenty-seven-year-old doctor who came on the trip to take care of Lord Milton.

Belly Ache was a difficult, older schoolteacher whose real name was Eugene Francis O'Beirne. At Fort Edmonton, he met Lord Milton and Dr. Cheadle and begged them take him over the mountains, because he had no money. He was such a troublemaker that the fur traders at Fort Edmonton gave him a free horse, just to get rid of him. The same thing had happened at Fort Pitt in what is now Saskatchewan.

The Battenotte family and the three adventurers left Fort Edmonton on April 28, 1863. A Métis guide named Baptiste Supernat travelled with them, but rode away at the McLeod River.

Dr. Cheadle often mentioned the Battenotte boy's bravery in his diary. The younger guide volunteered to swim across dangerous rivers to tie a rope that would guide the horses to safety. Once, when the deep, tumbling rapids of the Fraser River carried away two horses, he helped his father to rescue them.

The trip brought one disaster after another. The travellers almost drowned in the Fraser River, and saved themselves by throwing ropes over a tree branch and dragging themselves out of the water. When they ran out of food, they had to eat one of their horses to stay alive.

Exhausted and hungry, their clothes in rags, they arrived at Fort Kamloops on August 28, 1863. The boy's dog was skinny, but survived the trip too.

By this time the two Englishmen were ready to pay O'Beirne— old Belly Ache—to go away and never come back.

Dr. Cheadle gave the old man some socks, a silk necktie, tea, sugar, bread, and money. Lord Milton gave him more tea, tobacco, and matches. The people at Fort Kamloops gave him cakes and bacon.

When O'Beirne bellyached for more money, everybody refused. He moved to Australia and was never seen again.

Travelling west to the Pacific Ocean, the Battenotte boy had a lot of fun with his parents, Lord Milton and Dr. Cheadle when they reached Victoria. He rode around town in a fancy carriage, ate dinner with the governor, Sir James Douglas, and saw a musical play at the theatre. The Battenotte family also enjoyed a long sailing trip through the Gulf Islands with the two Englishmen before they said goodbye.

We don't know whether the boy ever returned to his home on the eastern side of the Rockies. How do you think he remembered his trip?

The Clark family: Lillian, the girl with the long hair, with
her parents and sister, about ten years before the Frank slide in 1903.

Where will I go?
Lillian Clark, age fifteen,
Frank, a mining town in the Crowsnest Pass, 1903

I have nobody left, and no home to call my own.

"Cry, dear," Miss Thornley whispered this morning. "A good cry will make you feel better."

How could she say such a foolish thing? I turned away from her spoonful of soup and her comfort. I closed my eyes to make her disappear. She tiptoed out of the tent, thinking I had fallen asleep. As if I could.

I will lie under the blanket on this cot all day. I will keep my eyes closed. If visitors lift the flap of the tent, I will ignore them. If I refuse to speak, maybe the police officer, the newspaper reporter, and that preacher will go away and never come back.

Their horrible questions come back to me every morning.

The police officer came first, unfolding his notebook. I pulled the blanket over my head, but he kept talking.

"Where were you, Lillian, on April 29? Why were you away from home? Could you tell me the names of your brothers and sisters? Was your father on shift working at the mine? Where was your mother? What did you hear, Lillian, when Turtle Mountain came crashing down?"

I heard the world crack open, that's what I heard. It was the sound of ten thousand thunderbolts. The cracking noise was so sharp, so sudden, that I sat up straight in bed, shrieking and cupping my hands over my ears. I felt a gust of icy wind. I saw a face I didn't recognize in the mirror, and then realized that the face was my own.

"Mama!" I called out, but no words came out of my throat. Was this a bad dream? It took me a long time to understand that I was waking up to my town's true nightmare.

It was the first night in my life I had slept away from home. I am trying to remember the way the day began.

Early in the morning, my mother packed my lunch and sent me on my way to my job as a maid at the boarding house.

She brought my scarf and hat. "If you finish your work very late tonight," she said, "ask your boss for a place to sleep until morning."

Her words surprised me. Every other day she had insisted that I walk straight home after work, no matter how tired I was, or how late the hour. Sometimes she came to meet me in the dark with a lantern.

I asked her why she had changed her mind.

"I didn't let you sleep there before, because I didn't trust the people who owned the boarding house," she said. "I think the new owners are good people. They won't hurt you. You can stay there tonight if you're sleepy."

I grabbed my lunch and kissed her goodbye. She smiled at the door. I waved to my brothers and sisters in the yard. I think I remember humming a tune as I walked down the lane.

I climbed the steps of the boarding house in the early morning to begin my day's work.

First I hauled six buckets of water from the pump in the yard.

I picked up the stinky chamber pots in each bedroom, dumped them in the outhouse, and scrubbed each one with a metal brush. I stripped each bed, washed the sheets on the scrub board in the yard, and pinned wet laundry to the clothesline. After that I carried the garbage and ashes from the wood stove to the dumping place in the alley. Then I scrubbed all the floors with a hard brush and a pail of soapy water. After that I peeled three dozen potatoes and three dozen carrots for the boarders' dinner at noon.

That was my morning.

"You can take a break now, Lillian," my boss said kindly. "Please be back in ten minutes."

Hungry and thirsty, I sat on the back step and ate my mother's soft raisin biscuits and a chunk of English cheese. I sipped a mug of sugary tea and lifted my face to the sunshine.

Then I began my afternoon work.

I washed, dried, and put away the dishes from the boarders' dinner. I polished the master's boots. I filled the woodbox with firewood. I fetched six more buckets of water from the pump. I swept the front steps and the back steps, and washed the coal dust from the windows in the parlour and kitchen. I plucked three chickens on the back step, and fetched beets from the cold cellar. Then I chopped cabbages and turnips for the boarders' supper. I took down the laundry from the line, and packed it into wicker baskets for ironing the next day.

At seven o'clock, I was plenty tired. I had finished the same chores every day except Sunday for many months, but I was still getting used to the idea that my workday would never change. Like Pa, going underground on the night shift, I knew what to expect.

"Thank you, Lillian," said my boss, coming out to the porch. "That will be enough for today. Would you care for a little warm soup?"

I shyly told her that my mother had given me permission to stay overnight if that would be alright with her. She showed me a room in the attic with a small bed. A kitten sat on a yellow quilt. I played with the kitten for a few minutes, and soon fell asleep in my clothes.

A few hours later, the world cracked open.

When the noise stopped, I heard frightened voices in the street. I jumped from my bed, pulled on my boots, and raced down the stairs as fast as my feet would carry me.

Men with lamps were running up and down the road in the foggy darkness, shouting to one another in wild voices. What confusion! Babies and small children wailed. Old people shouted that the end of the world had come.

Where was my family? I ran for my home, but never reached it. A wall of boulders blocked my path. Angrier than I had ever been, I pounded my fists on the rocks until I fell to the ground, sobbing. A weary man came and carried me away.

That is all I can remember of the night that Turtle Mountain tumbled down on my town. I have no more answers for anyone.

I can hear the voices of strangers, murmuring outside the tent.

"That's the poor Clark girl, in there," Miss Thornley is telling them. "When the mountain fell, her father died outside the mine entrance. Her mother and six little brothers and sisters died when the rocks fell on their house. As fortune would have it, Lillian was away for the night. The lucky girl. What a blessing."

This morning is no blessing. I will take a deep breath, and pray for sleep.

What do we know for sure?

Lillian Clark was the only member of her family to survive the Frank Slide on April 29, 1903. She was fifteen years old. She owed her life to her mother's decision to allow her to sleep overnight for the first time at the boarding house where she worked.

Just before dawn, at 4:10 that morning, 82 million tonnes of rock from Turtle Mountain tumbled down on the little mining town in the Crowsnest Pass.

The mountain had always been unstable. The Blackfoot and Ktunaxa, or Kootenay people, knew Turtle Mountain as "the mountain that moves," and some said they refused to camp near it. Coal mining weakened the mountain's structure, and in the spring of 1903, water seeped into the deep crevices, froze, and put extreme pressure on the shaky mountain. Finally, a huge wedge of limestone at the top cracked, broke into chunks—from little stones to boulders the size of a house, and slid down the mountainside on the people below.

About one minute later, an avalanche of shale and limestone poured down into the valley, missing the main part of the town, but burying the houses and buildings on the eastern side of Gold Creek, where Lillian's family lived.

It was one of the worst natural disasters in Canadian history. The town of Frank had about six hundred inhabitants, and one hundred of them lived in the path of the avalanche. About seventy

Townspeople examine the damage in Frank on
the day after the disaster in 1903.
GLENBOW ARCHIVES NA-586-2

people are believed to have been killed, although no one knows
the exact number.

Seventeen coal miners on the night shift were trapped underground for thirteen hours. They survived by digging through ten
metres of coal and limestone boulders. Unfortunately, Lillian's
father, Alfred Clark, had climbed to the mine entrance just before
4 AM to have something to eat with another miner. He was killed
in the landslide.

Lillian was the eldest daughter in her family. Her mother,
Amelia Clark, died with her six younger sons and daughters in
the family home.

Many other children and teenagers died in the town of Frank

that night, including John, Wilfred, Allan, and Athol Leitch; one Ackroyd child; the two Van Dusen children; two hired boys named Johnson, who worked for the Graham family; the seven Warrington children; and the three Williams children.

Miraculously, most of the twenty-three survivors in the worst-hit area of Frank's eastern flats were also children. They included Thomas, Fernie, and Ruby Watkins; Delbert, James, Arthur, Hazel, and Gladys Ennis; Lester Ackroyd; Marion, Jessie, and Rosemary Leitch; and Alex, Carl, Frances, Rose, Hilda, Kate, and Harold Bansemer.

After the slide, a rumour spread about a little baby girl discovered on a boulder. The story went that the townspeople didn't know the baby's name, so they called her Frankie Slide—and the legend became a song. This tale was not true, but as Laura Neilson Bonikowsky discovered in her research for the Canadian Encyclopedia, three small girls did survive the slide in odd ways.

One baby, Marion Leitch, just fifteen months old, was thrown from her house and found in a pile of hay. Fernie Watkins was discovered in the rubble. Gladys Ennis, just two years old, was found in the mud by her mother, Lucy, who thought she was dead and carried her home in a blanket. When the sad mother unwrapped the blanket, she saw signs of life and quickly cleared the mud out of her daughter's throat and nose. Little Gladys lived to be ninety-four years old; she was the last survivor of the Frank Slide when she died in 1995.

You can still see the huge landslide at Frank on Highway 3 in the Crowsnest Pass. To learn more, read William Kerr's excellent book *Frank Slide*, and be sure to visit the Frank Slide Interpretive Centre.

Elliott Barnes, Jr., on the summit of Elliott Peak, 1906.

King Elliott

Elliott Barnes, Jr., age eight,
at the top of Elliott Peak, 1906

Hey, you down there. I dare you to climb to the top of my mountain. I am the king of the castle, but I won't call you a dirty rascal. I want a friend up here. Come on up. We can make a fort and spy on the world.

You don't want to climb straight up? Why not? Are you afraid you might fall? Just hold on to the rocks, and watch where you put the toes of your boots. Don't huff and puff so much. Don't look down until you get to the top.

Look up at me instead. I climbed to the top of this mountain from our ranch down in the valley. My family didn't try to stop me. They knew I could get here on my own two feet, and I did.

Here is what I can see from up here.

I am so high in the sky that I can see the Great Wall of China and the pyramids of Egypt. I can see a red balloon flying over India. I can see three pirates burying gold on an island near Jamaica. I can see two puppies wrestling in Japan, and a polar bear dipping his nose into the Arctic Ocean. I can see kangaroos hopping in Australia, camels spitting in the Sudan, and penguins belly-flopping on the ice in Antarctica. I can see an African girl exactly my age sitting on the top of Mount Kilimanjaro. She is waving to me. I am waving back.

Are you still scared? Keep climbing. I am waiting for you.

I am so high in the sky that when I look up, I can see the sun and moon and all of the planets and stars. I can see clowns riding bicycles on Mars, and acrobats walking a tightrope on Pluto. I can see mice sliding on the rings of Saturn, and chimpanzees swinging from the Big Dipper. I can see a lantern in a sandcastle on the Milky Way. I can see knights in shining armour on Jupiter. I can see a solid gold tree house on Neptune.

You don't believe one word I say, do you? Well, climb up here and see for yourself. My mountain just might surprise you.

What do we know for sure?
Elliott Barnes, Jr., did climb to the top of a tall mountain in 1906, when he was eight years old. He was the first person known to have climbed to the peak.

His father, whose name was also Elliott Barnes, was climbing right behind him, and he took the photograph of his son at the summit.

You can probably guess the imaginary part of this story. We don't know what Elliott could see from the top of the mountain, but it is highly unlikely that he could see the penguins of Antarctica. The pirates, maybe.

We do know that the Canadian authorities named Elliott Peak in 1907 in honour of the young boy who dared to climb to the top. The mountain is also sometimes known as Mount Elliott.

You can see the mountain today if you are travelling on Highway 11 from Rocky Mountain House through the North Saskatchewan River valley, driving toward the mountains. The best place to see it is from the viewpoint above Abraham Lake.

In the summer of 1906, young Elliott was living on a ranch where his parents were raising purebred Clydesdale horses. His family called the ranch Kadonna Tina, which meant "windy plains" in the language of the Nakoda people, who lived all around them. The boy knew the children of Silas Abraham well, because the Nakoda family took care of the Barnes' ranch when they were away. You can read their story on page 89. Abraham Lake is named after this family.

Elliott's father left behind beautiful photographs of the people and places of the northern Rockies. You can see more pictures of his family and friends in a book called *A Delicate Wilderness: The Photography of Elliott Barnes, 1905–1914*, or in the larger collection at the Whyte Museum and Archives of the Canadian Rockies in Banff.

Elliott's father took many interesting pictures of children.

The boy moved with his family to another ranch near Calgary when he was a little older. Young Elliott liked the mountains, but the Clydesdale horses didn't, so his parents decided to move.

In 1967, the year Canada celebrated its one hundredth birthday as a nation, Elliott Barnes, Jr., decided to climb Elliott Peak again as his own centennial project. He was sixty-nine years old. He brought along several of his children and grandchildren. Once again, he made it all the way to the peak.

Paul Sharpless on Maligne Lake, 1911.

The Rocky Mountain cure

Paul Sharpless, age nine,
Maligne Lake, 1911

If you ever want a big adventure in the Rocky Mountains, I advise you to get a whopping case of whooping cough.

It worked for me.

I never would have travelled to the Rockies—or had a mountain named after me—if I hadn't been so sick last winter. I coughed and coughed and coughed. My parents worried all day and all night. I stopped eating. I was never hungry.

I am the only child in my family, so grown-ups fluttered around my bed like pigeons. They made cooing noises. That didn't help my health any.

We live in Philadelphia, Pennsylvania, USA. in a great, big old house with many rooms. When my mother heard me cough, she came running to my bedroom with a spoonful of cod liver oil. Have you ever tasted that gooey stuff? I jumped out of bed and raced from room to room to get away, but she always caught up with me. "Open your mouth! Wide! Swallow!"

Cod liver oil made me burp, but it did not make me better. The doctor came and gave me medicine that tasted like dirt syrup. Then a gaggle of aunts came to the house to give my mother their best advice on a cure.

"Paul looks so tired and frail," one aunt said. "He needs to rest in bed all day with the curtains closed."

"Paul looks so pale and nervous," another aunt said. "He needs quiet Sunday drives in the country. Strictly no excitement."

"Paul looks so thin and weak," a third aunt said. "He needs a large dose of molasses three times a day."

I was sure their cures were going to kill me.

Aunt Mary strode into my bedroom just in time. She calls herself my No Nonsense Aunt. She took a long look at me—tired, feeble, pale, nervous, thin, and weak—and she looked down at the supper tray beside my bed. I hadn't touched the barley soup. I hadn't sipped one drop of the carrot juice that the doctor had suggested.

"I know a far better cure, if the family will agree," she told my mother and aunts. "Let me take him to a land where they never have coughs, where it is just ponies and swimming, bears and fishing, fresh air and fried bacon." She said she could guarantee that I would come home to Philadelphia with new strength that would surprise my doctor.

Aunt Mary is an explorer, an adventurer, a botanist, a writer, and a wildflower painter. She goes to the Canadian Rockies every summer to search for interesting plants and places. She told me she needed my help with a map she was making of a beautiful lake high in the mountains.

"You will ride a pack horse with me and two mountain guides, Mr. Unwin and Mr. Otto, and their helpers," she said. "We will build a raft to explore the lake once we get there. How does that sound, Paul?"

I just smiled at her. I liked the sound of her cure.

My parents agreed to the plan, but my mother insisted on

coming along to take care of me. For the next few weeks, we filled my duffle bag for the trip. Here is what I packed:

a corduroy suit
a cowboy hat
an old suit in case I fell in the water
a huge knife
a jackknife
a flaming red silk neckerchief like the fellows in the West wear
sweaters
rain poncho
new hobnailed boots for climbing mountains
leather leggings
warm long underwear
my camera

As soon as summer came, Aunt Mary and Mama and I climbed on the train and began our journey. First we travelled across the border into Canada. In Montreal, we climbed on another train that took us through empty forests, and over flat prairies, for days and days of card games. I played Mumblety Peg, Buzz, and One-Horned Lady until I was cross-eyed. To keep myself busy, I also planned how I would build the raft.

We finally stopped in a dusty town called Edmonton and found out that Aunt Mary's trunk and my duffle bag were far behind us. I was very sad about going to the mountains without a jackknife and a cowboy hat. Trying to make me feel better, my mother bought me a butterfly net, a pair of suspenders, and the ugliest hat I had ever seen in my life.

It was a city-boy hat, not an explorer's hat. Mama put that

nasty thing on my head before we climbed on the last rickety train going toward the mountains. "It will keep the sun off your face, dear," she said.

Blasted hat!

I hated that hat so much that I stuck my head out of the train window, and the wind blew it off by accident. Then I had a bit of bad luck. A passenger named Tom hopped off the back of the caboose to fetch the hat for me! Running as fast as he could, he jumped back on the train, with that lumpy brown cap in his hand. My mother treated Tom like a hero. I stuck my tongue out at him, and then I got caught.

We finally got off the train in a little muddy place. Everywhere I looked, railway workers were staring at me. I knew it was because I looked foolish in my city-boy hat.

"Hullo there, lad!"

I looked up into the friendly eyes of a big stranger. It was our guide, Mr. Otto. He wore cowboy boots, leather chaps, a big wide-brimmed hat, and the friendliest smile in Canada. Mr. Otto lifted me onto a rough wagon, pulled by two big horses. We jolted and bounced over a bumpy trail. Every time the wagon hit a rock or fallen branch, I went flying, but Mr. Otto caught me before I tumbled to the ground.

Finally, I saw our first camp in the distance. I jumped down from the wagon and raced to see the inside of the tipi where I would sleep. Then I ran to the campfire, where our supper was soon sizzling and sputtering in Mr. Otto's frying pan. Can you believe that I forgot I was sick? I gulped down bacon, potatoes, peas, and fruitcake with jam.

"Could I have some more?" I asked.

"Sure, lad," said Mr. Otto.

The next morning, my mother told me to brush my teeth and wash the grime from my face. I pointed to Mr. Otto.

"He never washes, and I won't either," I said. For once, she couldn't think of a word to say.

A few minutes later, Mr. Otto brought a beautiful horse toward me. "This will be your friend, lad," he said. I took the halter and looked straight into the horse's brown eyes. The horse put down his nose and sniffed me. Mr. Otto told my mother and Aunt Mary that it was a gentle old roan that would carry me safely up into the mountains, but as he lifted me to the saddle, he whispered: "He bucked a grown man two days ago, boy, but I know you're big enough to ride him."

I was too excited to be nervous. I called my wild horse Roany. Mr. Otto showed me how to use the reins to guide him gently along the trail, and how to duck to avoid tree branches. I had never been on a horse before, but Mr. Otto said I was a strong rider.

One day, a blackfly bit Roany on the butt. Roany jumped a bit on purpose, so that my ugly brown hat could fly off my head and land on the trail. My horse moved backward and stomped on it with his strong back legs, then galloped forward to leave that awful hat in the Alberta dirt.

Thank you, Roany.

My horse did have his bad days. He would not budge when I tried to coax him to cross the Athabasca River. I guess he hates swimming in deep, dangerous water. The other horses stayed on the riverbank too, so Mr. Otto and Sid had to pull them into the water by their halters. Finally, they crossed the river, snorting and blowing, in a bad temper.

I understood why the horses were so mad when I tried swimming the next day. "That's the last bath I'll take in any of these cold lakes," I told Aunt Mary. "They look alright, but they're cold!"

Sometimes we rode nine hours in a day before we stopped to camp. I did stop once to explore the log ruins of the old Jasper House fur-trading fort.

Once, Roany and I met a black bear who was tearing up a rotten log to search for ants. I was so surprised, I just hollered: "Well, I declare!" The bear thought I was cuckoo, and ran away.

We were starting to climb very steep mountain trails that curved back and forth to the sky. I felt kind of sorry for Mr. Otto. He had the tough job of bringing the boards for our raft on the pack horses. A horse named Jonas did the hardest work, panting and puffing as he pulled the boards up the mountain.

At last, we reached the top of the trail. I was kind of dizzy and excited. Looking down, I could see the Athabasca River, and I counted thirty-two lakes in the valleys. All around me I saw hundreds of mountain peaks.

"See that one over there?" Mr. Otto pointed to a higher mountain covered with snow. "That's the one we have to cross tomorrow. Get your rest tonight, lad. You're going to need it."

I never thought I would wade through snow in the middle of July. The trail was twisting and dangerous, along the side of a steep cliff, and Roany was scared of falling. So I jumped down and led him by the halter rope, whispering: "Come on now, boy. We're almost there."

Snow filled my boots, and fell from the tree branches down the neck of my sweater. My sleeves were full of snow. I was cold, tired, and wet, but I didn't stop walking. Roany followed me because he trusted me.

We found two handmade shovels against a tree, left by some other trail riders to dig out their horses, stuck in the snow. I named this trail Shovel Pass.

The last day on the trail down to the lake was the hardest. The bush was thick and tangled. Poor Jonas struggled to carry the raft boards across a deep mountain stream. Mr. Otto called out to me: "Come back here, kid, and give me a lift." Roany carried both of us across the stream, but then the hard climbing began up the side of a steep riverbank. I got scared and started to sing a song called "My wife, she's gone to the country." Just to calm Roany, you understand.

"You will never see your wife again if you don't watch where you're riding," Mama told me. I paid no attention, and kept searching the valley below for the place we had come to see.

"I see the lake! Say, she's a dandy!"

Mr. Otto said the lake was still about five miles away, and we had difficult rapids to cross first. When we reached the riverbank, Jonas the horse stumbled, falling with all the raft boards, and his head went right under the water. Mr. Otto jumped into the rapids to save him from drowning. Mr. Unwin chased the floating boards. I tried to jump over the stream, but I tumbled into the water too, and somebody fished me out. I was still soaking wet when we finally reached the lake.

Have you ever seen Maligne Lake? It looks like a magic lake.

Paul Sharpless rowing the *HMS Chaba the Second* with his guide in 1911.

The best part of my adventure started that day. As soon as we set up our tipis on the lakeshore, we began to build the raft. I did everything that Aunt Mary and Mr. Unwin and Mr. Otto asked me to do. Hammered nails. Jammed gooey stuff called oakum into the cracks. Smeared the raft with pitch so it wouldn't leak. Finally, the raft was ready for her first voyage.

"What are we going to call her, Aunt Mary?" I asked.

"I don't know," she said. "Samson Beaver and his family call this lake *Chaba Imne*," she said. "Three summers ago, we built a raft here and I called it the *HMS Chaba*."

I remembered my great idea and ran away to the cook tent.

"Hurry up, buster; we're going to launch her!" Mr. Otto hollered after me. "You don't want to miss it!"

I had been hiding an old vinegar bottle for this moment. I searched everywhere in the cook tent, but it was gone! "Don't worry," my mother said. "I've been using it as a rolling pin. Here you go."

I ran back to the lake, filled the bottle with water, and smashed it into a thousand pieces against the front of the raft, just like the King of England would do with an ocean ship.

"I christen thee His Majesty's Ship, *Chaba the Second*!" I yelled. My voice echoed back across the lake. It sounded happy.

I almost forgot there was a place called Philadelphia after that. One day we heard a shout from the other end of the lake, and my old life came chasing after me. Bruce, another trail guide, appeared with my duffle bag from the train station in Edmonton. Quickly, I pulled everything out of the bag. I found my jackknife, cowboy hat, red neckerchief, shirt, and breeches. I got dressed right on the shore. I didn't look like an orphan anymore in Aunt Mary's old jacket.

With all my stuff, I could live beside Maligne Lake forever.

Some days, Mr. Otto and I row our raft along the shore for Aunt Mary when she measures the lake. I chase mountain gophers and try to trap them in little loops of string.

One day an eagle swooped down and tried to grab me by the collar, but I ran away. Another day I went hunting with Mr. Otto for a mountain goat for our supper.

I take pictures of ducks and sandpipers with my camera. Mr. Otto showed me how to climb a mountain with ropes and picks. One morning I made a dam on a small stream to make a little lake.

Another day I picked wild onions for our supper. Later I slept on a blanket on the hard ground, outside the tipi, to watch the stars at night. The Man in the Moon winked at me over a mountain. In the mornings, Roany and I disappear to explore the woods on our own.

All of this hard work makes me hungry. Mr. Unwin and Mr. Otto brought a small camp oven for baking bread and pies, and we cook almost everything else in frying pans over the campfire. I was happy when Mr. Otto said he had never heard of carrot juice. As for barley soup, he said grain is for horses.

"Yer Philadelphia whooping cough food doesn't sound too delicious," he told me. "Does yer doctor eat it?"

One night at Maligne Lake, I ate most of a wild duck. The next morning, I ate raisin pie for breakfast. The night after that, I ate hot biscuits, corn, beans, and fried ham. The day after Independence Day, I ate wild duck, partridges stuffed with wild onions, and one whole loaf of bread.

The next night, I ate macaroni and cheese, fried ham, potatoes, fried mush, rice pudding, and apple pie for supper, and then I got hungry before I went to bed, so I ate Johnny cake, fried potatoes and jam. The day after that I ate tomato stew, fried potatoes, shintangle pudding, and another loaf of bread. And the next night, I ate two loaves of bread full of raisins, currants, and cinnamon, and also a currant pie, boiled beans, fried farina, cakes, chipped beef, and more pie.

On the day Mr. Otto came back with the goat, I also ate stuffed grouse and duck, prune pie and apple water, Brown Betty, roast partridge, and baked beans. My mouth was too busy eating to cough.

Sometimes it is hard to go to bed after Mr. Otto's scary stories beside the campfire. I listen for coyotes, wolves, and bears prowling around in the dark. One night I heard a scratch, scratch, scratch on the side of the tipi, and I knew it was a bear.

I heard Aunt Mary whisper to Mama: "Carrie, does thee hear a noise?"

I heard Mama whisper to Aunt Mary: "It is a beast of some kind."

I could hardly sleep, I was so scared. When I crawled out of the tent in the morning, I saw that the mountain wind had dumped heavy snow all over our camp. The frightening noise had only been the snow chunks falling from tree branches and sliding down the outside of our tipi. With a frying pan, I dug a path through the snow to the cook tent.

"Are you going to name all these mountains, Aunt Mary?" I asked a few days later, when the sun came out again.

"Some of them, I suppose," she said.

"Am I too little to have a mountain named after me?"

She saw me staring up at the tallest peaks.

"If you promise me you will get up in time for breakfast, fetch wood for the campfire, and eat up your dinner every night when you get back to Philadelphia, I will call that mountain peak over there Mount Paul. Remember that if you fail to keep your part of the bargain, off comes the name."

She kept her promise. I kept mine. Aunt Mary's cure for the whooping cough is the best medicine in the world.

What do we know for sure?

At the age of nine, Paul Sharpless travelled with his adventurous aunt, Mary Schäffer, and his mother, Caroline Sharpless, from Philadelphia, Pennsylvania, in the United States to Maligne Lake in Jasper National Park in western Canada.

Their summer adventure lasted from May 28, 1911 until August 16, 1911. They travelled with their mountain guides, Sid Unwin and Jack Otto, several other men, and twelve horses, including Paul's loyal horse, Roany.

If you visit Maligne Lake today, you can see Mount Paul at the southern end of the valley, in the Queen Elizabeth Range.

We know a lot about the trip because Paul's Aunt Mary Schäffer wrote books, journals, and lectures about her explorations. She also wrote an unpublished story about Paul's experiences, called *An American Boy's Summer in the Canadian Rockies*, which is now in the archives of the Whyte Museum of the Canadian Rockies in Banff. Paul's mother wrote a detailed diary of the trip, and carefully noted everything they ate each day. She was very worried about Paul's health, but she was also very proud of him.

Almost all of the words spoken by the characters in this story come from books and manuscripts at the Whyte Museum and Archives. The parts about Paul's whooping cough, his aunt's cure, and all of the other details in the story are all in the diaries—except that nobody knows for certain how Paul got rid of the ugly brown hat. The author guessed that Roany tried to help his young pal.

Mary Schäffer was a Philadelphia Quaker who came to the Rockies for the first time when she was eighteen years old. She married a much older American botanist. After he died in 1903, she continued to come to the Rockies to paint wildflowers and to explore the wilderness with her friends Mollie Adams and Mary Vaux. In 1904, a five-year-old girl travelled with them.

One day in 1907, Mary Schäffer met a Nakoda family— Samson Beaver, his wife Leah, and their daughter, Frances Mary. Samson told her about a hidden lake in a faraway valley that he had visited with his father when he was fourteen years old. He called the lake *Chaba Imne*, and drew a map for her to follow.

Excited about the challenge, Mary visited Maligne Lake for the first time in 1908, and published a book about her many adventures, now available under the title *A Hunter of Peace*. She returned in 1911 with Paul to learn more about the lake, and to take measurements for accurate mapping. Mary Schäffer married her favourite trail guide, Billy Warren, in 1915, and lived for the rest of her life in the town of Banff. She died in 1939.

We know little about what happened to Paul Sharpless after he returned home to Philadelphia with his mother. His Aunt Mary wrote a letter in 1935—during the hard times of the Depression—and mentioned that her nephew had lost his job at Bell Telephones in New York. He and his wife and child had moved in with his parents to save money.

We don't know if Paul ever visited the Rockies again, but his name stayed on Mount Paul. The handmade shovels that Paul found on the snowy trail are on display at the Jasper Yellowhead Museum and Archives. The mountain pass is still called Shovel Pass.

Somewhere along the trail, Paul carved his initials and the date on a tree trunk. Perhaps his carved message—P.S. 1911—is still visible at the very top of an old, old tree.

Silas Abraham and an unidentified son.

Come ride with us

The children of Silas and Gussie Abraham,
Hector Crawler, and another man named
Abraham, at the Iyarhe Nakodabi camp,
Bighorn River, 1912

We are watching a young stranger. We can see she is smiling.

The girl is taller than us, but she looks shy. She is wearing a long dark skirt, a dark shirt, a dark floppy hat, and dark boots. Her riding gloves are too big for her small hands.

Aba washded, we say. Good day to you. *Dudiki naca*. Where are you going?

The girl doesn't answer. She shrugs her shoulders.

We whisper to each other. Is she a teacher from Morley? No, she is younger than a teacher. She is only a little older than us. How can you tell? Look, she doesn't tie her hair up yet. Why is her skirt divided in two for each of her legs? Why does she wear boots that belong to a man? Is she a boy?

The little kids are giggling, but Silas's son hushes them.

"*Ade* told me she's the daughter of his friend, Nordegg," he says. "Listen, she's starting to talk to us."

The strange girl opens her mouth. She speaks a language we have never heard. It isn't English like the teachers in Morley speak. It isn't the French of the old priest who visits us on his big horse. It isn't Cree or Blackfoot either. We don't understand one word she says.

We ask her so many questions. Where did you come from? Why are you travelling without your mother? How old are you? Why do you wear teachers' clothes, and a skirt divided in two? Do those boots hurt your feet?

The girl looks at us. She shakes her head back and forth. She touches her ears to give us a message.

Silas's son understands. "She is trying to tell us she doesn't understand our language," he explains. "Look over there. That must be her horse. Do you think she would like to ride with us while her father talks with *Ade* at the camp?"

We all start to talk about his idea. Where will we take her? What will we show her?

The older sisters say the girl looks thin and hungry. Maybe they don't have enough food in her country. Should we ride with her to the place where we pick deep-blue huckleberries? Or low-bush cranberries? We wonder which juicy taste she would like best.

The little brothers say the girl looks cold in her dark clothes. Maybe they don't have enough sunshine in her country. Should we take her up the mountain to see the summer buttercups? Or yellow paintbrush? Or wild orange poppies? Should we ride with her to the place where blue butterflies and green dragonflies play tag above the wild roses?

The little sisters say the girl looks lonely beside her father and the old men. Maybe they don't have enough brothers and sisters in her country. Should we race on our horses on the river flats with her? Should we take her to the caves where the bats fly? Should we ride to the rapids to watch for golden trout? Or to the rocks to search for a painted turtle or a red-sided snake or a yellow

The Iyarhe Nakodabi camp at the Bighorn River on the
day of the visit in 1912.

and black salamander or a spotted toad?

The older brothers say the girl looks like she needs to have
more fun. Maybe they don't laugh enough in her country. Should
we take her up to the cliffs to search for the little animals that
play with us? The meadow jumping mice and the voles? The red-
tailed chipmunks and the flying squirrels? Should we teach her
how to chase marmots? Will she laugh if she sees a squeaking pica
or a waddling porcupine?

We whisper to each other about our plans. The girl watches
us. She turns to listen to each of our voices.

Silas's son tells us that she is travelling over the mountains.
When will she leave? *Hakijhi.* Tomorrow.

"We should we take her to the high trail," he says, "so she can look down at all the lakes, rivers, and forests in our territory before she goes away."

He walks toward the girl, points to her horse, then points up to our mountains. He asks her to ride with us.

For the second time, she shakes her head.

"I don't think she will ever understand us," says Silas's son. "When *Ade* told us she was coming here, *Ina* made her a gift to take along on her trip across the mountains. Watch me. I'm going to give it to her now."

He walks toward the girl. He is holding out a gift in his hands that she can take away to remember us. We watch her face, and wait for her smile.

— — —

What do we know for sure?

The children of three Iyarhe Nakodabi families gave their gifts to a fourteen-year-old German girl named Marcelle Nordegg at a camp at the mouth of the Bighorn River in August 1912.

We know what happened that day because the girl's father, Martin Nordegg, described the meeting in his diary, and in a large album he made for his daughter about their trip. He also took pictures with a camera.

You'll find Marcelle's side of this story in the next chapter.

Iyarhe Nakodabi means the Mountain People, and this is what they call themselves. English-speaking people more commonly use the words Stoney, Stoney Nakoda, or Nakota to describe their community. In their language, *Ade* means father and *Ina* means mother.

We don't know the names of all the children who were on the riverbank that day. We do know some of their parents' names; Hector Crawler, Silas Abraham and Gussie Abraham, and another man whose first name was Abraham.

Hector Crawler became a respected chief later in his life. Silas Abraham was an experienced guide who helped newcomers like Martin Nordegg, Mary Schaffer, Elliott Barnes, Sr., and Tom Wilson find their way through the foothills and mountains.

Visiting the Abraham family's winter cabin, another hunter, Samson Beaver, drew his famous map of *Chaba Imne*, later called Maligne Lake, based on his childhood memories of exploring the mountains with his father. Today you can see Mount Samson and Mount Leah, named for Samson and his wife, on Maligne Lake in Jasper National Park.

Abraham Lake is named after the family of Silas Abraham.

Many photographs of these families were taken at their camps near the Kootenay Plains between 1900 and 1914. The pictures can teach us a lot about their traditions and way of life. Thousands of their family members live in Alberta today.

The Iyarhe Nakodabi are descendants of the great Sioux nations. Their historic territory is in the foothills on the eastern side of the Rocky Mountains. Traditionally, they hunted, fished, trapped, and traded for their livelihood.

Three chiefs, Jacob Bearspaw, John Chiniki or Chiniquay, and Jacob Goodstoney, brought their bands into Treaty 7 after discussions with representatives of the British Crown at Blackfoot Crossing in September 1877.

In their history of their community, published on their web

site, the descendants describe the treaty as "a sacred, living agreement that was intended to create a relationship of trust, mutual respect, and cooperation between our people and the Crown . . . In exchange for our peace and friendship, the Crown formally recognized us as independent Nations, and agreed to secure our traditional self-government, economy, and way of life."

According to the agreement in the peace treaty, the Iyarhe Nakodabi claimed a reserve of 109 square miles at Morley, on the Bow River between the Kananaskis and Ghost Rivers. The Bearspaw and Wesley-Goodstoney nations later claimed additional reserve land to the south and north. Much later, in 1948, the Bighorn reserve, Kiska Waptan, was established west of the community of Nordegg, and the Eden Valley reserve was established west of Longview.

To the north, the Alexis Nakota Sioux Nation and Paul's First Nation live in Treaty 6 territory—but they belong to the same Nakoda/Nakota Sioux Nation in Alberta.

You can learn more about the Iyarhe Nakodabi today by visiting their communities, or by reading their web sites www.stoneynation.com and www.alexisnakotasioux.com

The Nakoda Pow Wows are held every year at the Chief Goodstoney Rodeo Centre at Morley.

The summer of my happiness

Marcelle Nordegg, age fourteen,
Bighorn River, August 1912

The children are walking toward me. I can see they are smiling. They are younger than me, and shy like me too. They are whispering to each other. I don't understand one word they say.

The little ones giggle and hide their smiles behind their hands. An older boy is talking to me. I can tell he wants me to go somewhere, because he keeps pointing to his horse and my horse. I shake my head to tell them I don't know what to do.

The oldest boy turns around to look at his mother, who is standing beside her tipi. When she nods, he walks slowly toward me.

The boy puts a gift into my hand. It is a soft leather bag, made of elk skin, and decorated on the front with delicate blue and red beads. So beautiful. When I hold it up to my face, I notice a faint perfume of woodsmoke and spruce forest that I can take home with me.

I bow to them, and tie it to my waist.

Then the boy comes back with a second gift. He reaches up and puts a long necklace of the softest deer hide around my neck. At the end of the necklace, a tiny bag full of a sweet-smelling grass swings back and forth in the sunlight.

His mother is trying to explain something to me. She touches the tiny bag and then strokes my cheek, talking in a soft, kind

Marcelle Nordegg with pups a few days before her visit
to the Iyarhe Nakodabi camp in 1912.
COURTESY OF JOHN KOCH

voice. I look into her eyes. I think she can tell that I don't understand her words. She smiles and walks away.

"*Danke schön,*" I say. Thank you.

I tell the boy and the younger children that this is the most
exciting summer I can remember. I love their Rocky Mountains,
their forests, their sunlight, their strong horses, their warm tipis,
their wild Saskatchewan River, their cooking fires, the delicious

trout in their creeks, and most of all, their blue, blue sky.

"If I could live with you forever, I would," I tell them. "Wherever I go, I will remember you."

I promise them that I will come back again next summer with many presents from Germany. A wooden puppet. A cuckoo clock. A bicycle. A doll with a china face and ringlets. A toy drum.

"My papa will pack everything in a trunk, and we will bring our gifts back just for you, in a ship over the Atlantic Ocean, on a train to Rocky Mountain House, on pack horses through Nordegg, to your camp. We will meet you on your Kootenay Plains."

They are looking at one another, and shrugging their shoulders. They don't understand me either.

I want to give them a gift right away, and not wait for another summer. But what do I have in my saddlebag?

Nothing seems good enough. I have one tin of sardines in tomatoes, one tin of apricots, and a bag of dried pea soup in the shape of a sausage. I have my woolen hat, my raincoat, and my long underwear. I have a dirty, worn-out pair of leather boots. Not one good gift.

Then I remember the chocolate.

Papa packed many bars of the best German chocolate for our trip. He wrapped them in layers of newspaper and tucked them into his saddlebag. He told me the chocolate would keep me happy if we had to ride for ten hours through rain or snow on a high mountain trail.

We have two parcels of chocolate left for the rest of our ride across the mountains.

I run to Papa's horse, and dig through his saddlebag until I find my treasure. I also find a full tin of cocoa powder.

Maybe these children have already tasted Canadian chocolate, but German chocolate is different. I think they will like it.

Speaking with my hands, I tell them to follow me to their cooking fire. I fill their tea kettle with water and put it on the fire. I put some cocoa powder in the bottom of a tin bowl, add a splash of water, and stir the mixture into a paste with a willow stick. Then I add the bubbly hot water from the kettle.

They are watching me closely. They sniff the bowl. The oldest boy lifts a pretend mug to his lips to drink. He seems to be asking me a question.

I blow on my hand, and shake my head quickly to tell him that the cocoa is too hot to drink yet.

Then I unwrap the chocolate bar from the layers of newspaper, and take my jackknife out of my skirt pocket. I count the children, and carefully cut the chocolate into pieces so that each child will have a little taste of Germany.

I use my hands again to talk. I pick up a pretend piece of chocolate with one finger and dip it into a pretend bowl of warm cocoa. Then I swallow, smile, and rub my stomach to show them the chocolate will taste good.

They come closer to see. The real chocolate pieces are melting a bit on the rock. One girl touches a sticky piece, wrinkles her nose, and shakes her head. I use my hands to tell the others to give it a try, and then even the shy girl comes forward.

They dip. They taste. Their eyes sparkle.

In this one sparkling moment, the world is perfect.

They are saying new words to me.

Now we are sitting on their riverbank, searching for frogs. We take turns sipping the last of the hot cocoa.

"It is time to go, *mein liebes Kind*," Papa says, coming to find me. "My dear child, I won't leave without you."

I don't want to leave them, I tell him. With a smile, he lifts me up to Tibby's saddle. I push my feet into the stirrups and take the reins.

The children are watching me.

I touch the tiny bag on the necklace around my neck, and the beaded elk-hide bag tied to my waist. Then I kiss my cocoa-stained fingers, and wave to them.

"*Auf wiedersehen*," I say. "Goodbye. I will never forget you."

What do we know for sure?

Marcelle Nordegg said goodbye to the Iyarhe Nakodabi, or Stoney Nakoda, children that day in the late summer of 1912, hoping to return to see them again. Sadly, she never came back to the Rockies.

Marcelle met the families at the mouth of the Bighorn River. It was her second visit to the Rocky Mountains with her father, Martin Nordegg, a wealthy German businessman who had fallen in love with the Canadian wilderness.

Martin made many friends among the Nakoda people, and among the early cattle ranchers, who guided him through the foothills in his search for a good place to build a coal mine and a mining town. He called his chosen town Nordegg, and named a street after his adventurous daughter, Marcelle.

Marcelle did not speak the Nakoda language, and her new friends could not speak German, but they liked each other.

We know that because her father kept a diary of Marcelle's long journey from Toronto to Edmonton to Rocky Mountain House and Nordegg, along the North Saskatchewan River and then through the Pipestone Pass to Laggan, the old name for Lake Louise. They ended their Canadian trip in Vancouver.

Later, Martin made a keepsake gift for his daughter. He typed the story, added photographs and pressed wildflowers, and bound it in a big leather-covered album.

Martin's book explains that the Nakoda children gave Marcelle the elk-hide beaded bag and the necklace with the little bag of sweetgrass, made for her by one of their mothers.

Martin's diary does not mention his daughter's gifts to the Nakoda children, so the present of German chocolate is a guess in this story. We do know that Martin offered his daughter the last chunk of delicious German chocolate on a difficult ride in the mountains a few days later.

Although Marcelle was homesick for her mother on her long journey, she had many adventures. All the men on the trip said she was an excellent rider. Marcelle rode her horse, Tibby, on steep trails right over the Rockies, through heavy snow, and saw many elk, deer, mountain sheep, and mountain goats. She stopped to fish for trout and explored fields of wildflowers. At night, she listened to the men tell exciting and funny stories in a tipi. She slept under heavy blankets and coats on a bed of spruce boughs. She was very brave when she and her father travelled through a difficult and tangled forest for many hours.

"Often we heard the muffled growling of bears that lurked close to the camp," her father wrote, "and sometimes the shrieking of elks, the grunting of stags, and the strange calling of [moose] cows. Occasionally one heard the hissing and screaming of lynx and the whistling of marmots."

In 1995, John Koch, a writer in Edmonton of German background, found Marcelle's keepsake book when he was researching the life of Martin Nordegg. His wife, Maria Koch, carefully translated the story into English. You can read Marcelle's story in either language in the Kochs' book, *To the Town That Bears Your Name*.

Marcelle travelled around the world after she left the Rockies. First she went by ship from New York to Italy with her father, then she travelled to Egypt with her mother. A few years later, she moved to China, where she married an American man and had a baby boy.

She had a troubled life after that. She endured severe depression as a young woman. She divorced her husband, and left her son with him in China. She returned to Germany, where she began to suffer from acute schizophrenia in 1929.

Marcelle entered a private psychiatric clinic in Bonn in 1931 and lived there until 1944. The Kochs' careful research suggests that Marcelle was murdered in a government hospital in January, 1945, a few months before the end of the Second World War. She was forty-seven. Her body was buried in a mass grave. The Nazis who ruled Germany at that time killed people who were Jewish, and also people who were mentally ill. Marcelle was both.

Going showshoeing: (standing) Clifford White, Peter White,
Lila White, and Cyril Paris. (Sitting) Georgie Paris (?),
and Jackie White, in Banff, around 1910.

The great snowshoe leap

Peter White, age fifteen,
Banff, 1920

The moment Charlie shot the starting pistol, I sneezed.

Drat! The sneeze startled me. I stopped for a snitch of a second, and that gave Georgie his head start in the race.

He bolted toward the first obstacle fence through heavy snow. I was after him like a snowshoe rabbit with pepper in his nose.

The crowd lined our path, waiting for the first leap in the air. "Go, Pete!" "Go, Georgie!" "Go, Pete!" "Go, Georgie!"

The truth is, we had the same friends. They had to cheer for both of us.

You probably already know that it's hard enough to walk on snowshoes, let alone run and jump on the things.

At breakfast, my dad had repeated the rules of the race: "Remember, Peter, run in your own track. You have to run straight at the fence, and jump over it without tipping it or letting your snowshoes touch the wood. You are not allowed to hold the fence or throw both feet over it in the same direction. Jump one foot at a time."

Georgie had almost reached the first hurdle. I took deep breaths of ice-cold air as I ran to catch up.

The trick of snowshoeing is to tiptoe across the surface of the snow, without sinking down into the drifts. Snowshoes are so big that you keep stepping on top of your own feet. It is a bit like trying to run on giant dinner plates. You have to stretch your legs far apart.

If you trip, you can tumble face first into a snowdrift, or you can fall backward so that you are waving these huge clodhopper snowshoes up to the sky.

Georgie jumped, and he cleared the first fence. The crowd cheered. I was right behind him, and I jumped as if I had bedsprings under my toes. I made it over the barrier with a sliver of air to spare.

One jump behind us, six to go. The crowd was chanting again. I could hear my brother's voice calling to me, "Keep goin', Peter!"

Aaa—choo! Another sneeze! Georgie turned around to see what was happening.

I was right behind him, bursting with energy, and by mistake I stepped on the tail end of his left snowshoe. We both tumbled, and collapsed into the drifts. Georgie's toque came off. The crowd roared: "Lost his hat! Lost his hat!"

He got up and ran past me with a grin on his face—hatless.

As I struggled to my feet, the tip of my right snowshoe slid under the crust of snow, and tripped me again. The crowd shouted: "Pete, stand up! Pete, stand up!"

I could hear my brother's voice again, hollering: "For Pete's sake, Pete, stand up!"

Groaning, I pushed myself out of the snow. I stood up and started running again, just in time to see Georgie sail over the third fence.

I raced like I had an aeroplane engine inside my belly. Over the second fence! Over the third fence! Over the fourth fence!

All those weeks of practice began to pay off. I caught up to Georgie just after the sixth hurdle. We raced neck and neck to the last fence.

I could hear Georgie panting for breath. I knew he must be just as tired as me. Even though it was twenty-five below, I could feel sweat trickling down my spine. My shirt was soaked. My moccasins strained against the leather straps on my snowshoes. I didn't think I could take another aching step.

"Go! Last jump! Go!"

The crowd cheered wildly. From the corner of my eye, I could see my friends jumping and waving their arms in the air.

Here comes the fence. Georgie sailed through the air like a golden eagle. I took a flying leap right beside him.

Suddenly, I felt another sneeze on its way. Double-drat!

Aaa—CHOO!

Georgie tripped and I tumbled. All tangled up, we rolled together across the finish line.

Who won the race? Georgie said he did. I said I did. Everybody else in Banff told us they could only see four wild snowshoes in a whirl of snow, all flying in different directions.

Next year I'll stick to ski jumping.

What do we know for sure?

As a boy, Peter White was an excellent athlete in winter mountain sports. Born in 1905, he was the son of Dave White and Annie Curran White, who ran one of Banff's early stores.

Like many children in Banff in those days, Peter learned how to snowshoe as a small child. George Paris—the father of Georgie in this story—brought the first set of skis to Banff in 1894, but they broke on the first run.

Peter loved races of every kind, so he must have been delighted when the Banff Winter Carnival began.

You can learn more about the Banff Winter Carnival in two wonderful books by Alberta historian E.J. Hart, called *The Place of Bows* and *The Battle for Banff*.

Hart describes how skis came to Banff. To prepare for the first carnival in 1917, local boys made their own hardwood skis, using one part of round cheese boxes for the tips. They attached leather harnesses to hold their moccasins to the rough skis, and used broom handles for ski poles. The next year, Peter's father sold proper wooden skis in his store.

In 1918, young boys asked the park superintendent for permission to clear a slope on Mount Norquay. The superintendent agreed, but he asked them not to cut down every tree. They left one pine—and this became the legendary Lone Pine run, used mostly for snowshoeing until after the Second World War.

The Banff Winter Carnival was a magical time for children and adults alike. The Canadian Pacific Railway brought passengers on special trains from Winnipeg, Edmonton, and Vancouver for the carnival. Businesses in Banff donated trophies and prizes.

Young athletes could compete in snowshoe racing, dog sled racing, ski racing and jumping, figure skating, and skating races. In one race, a horseback rider would pull a skier, who would hold onto a rope attached to the horse's saddle. The festival also featured ice boating on Lake Minnewanka.

The sneeze is the imaginary part of this story, but we do know that Peter participated in the snowshoe obstacle race in 1920, because a photograph of the race survived.

Aside from snowshoe racing, Peter enjoyed exciting toboggan races on the long, slippery slide that started on Tunnel Mountain, ran down Cariboo Street, and ended up on the frozen Bow River. He won many prizes for his ski jumping on the Grizzly Street ski jump. Photographs of his childhood also show him competing in dog sled races, and helping to deliver the Banff mail on a dog sled.

Peter also loved to draw cartoons as a child. When he grew up, he left Banff briefly to study art in the United States. He changed the spelling of his family name to Whyte when he became a grown-up. While in the US he married another artist, Catharine Robb, and the couple moved back to the Rockies. They lived in Banff—hiking and skiing and painting together—for the rest of their lives.

Many years after the snowshoe race, Peter and Catharine Whyte helped another boy named Peter who came to Banff. You can read that story, "My war in the mountains", on page 153.

To learn more about this interesting family, and Banff's history, be sure to visit the Peter and Catharine Whyte Museum and Archives at 111 Bear Street in Banff. The friendly archivists there helped with many of the stories in this book.

Crag & Canyon

YOUR ADDRESS LABEL TELLS WHEN YOUR SUBSCRIPTION EXPIRES.

Banff, Alberta, Friday October 23rd, 1925 $2.00 Per Year

Band Concert In Lux Theatre Sun.

The Banff Citizens' Band, under the direction of Prof. A. Bagley, will give a band concert at the Lux Theatre on Sunday evening next, October 25th, at nine o'clock.

A good program of music which appears below, has been arranged and it is hoped that a good attendance will be present.

The endeavour is the first concern they are have been out what they should be and the Crag & Canyon understands that the band suffered a defeat at their debut in their last concert. Surely any growth and possible means for remit worth of enjoyment, so why not show your appreciation of good music by giving accordingly. If the concert was held once a week night and you were asked to pay twenty-five cents admission they would gladly pay it. Kindly keep your full fund in sight to assume, or must have funds to carry on and thus are not doing something for nothing.

The program for Sunday's concert is as follows:

1. March "Sampson Fidelio" Somes
2. Selection "Forester" Somerset May Hawthorne etc.
3. Post Valse "Emerald
4. Solo Violin "Lighthouse Baker" Arthur "Cape Solomon" from Arthur Major Forster soloist, Mr. Hubert Cow
5. Vocal Selection
6. Plantation Episode "Cross in the Cotton" Millie Hall
7. "South Sea" Bonnie Scotland
8. March "United Mexican" Lincoln "God save the King."

was for our country, and another way for another. Repair the town and inevitable may repeat the effect.

No country in the world is more blessed than Canada with the things necessary for rapid and sustained progress. All the needs is men and money in due time but its resources. And these she can get if she goes after them properly.

Being still what is commonly known a pioneer country, Canada should be attracting population from lands that are more congested. But at present she isn't. And the reason she isn't, is that she is doing nothing to assure the prosperity immigrant a steady job at good wage.

You Cannot Make Bricks Without

Grand Matron O. E. S. Visits Here.

WORTHY GRAND MATRON of S.A. VISITS BANFF CHAPTER

Canada Chapter, Order of the Eastern Star, was honoured on its official visit of the Worthy Grand Matron at their Order, Mrs. [illegible], presided on its Chapter on Monday evening last, October 19th.

During the visit Mrs. [illegible] was the guest of Mrs. Dora Rae, who has a most efficient officer.

The Canada Chapter Matron, Mrs. Sara Swift, gave a delightful review of the history of the Order, Mrs. John Thompson, who is hard pressed for finance, has the occasion. Above every fine intention of the music were on the way the staff to assume thematic selection.

[remaining columns illegible]

Three Local Girls Lost On Mountain; Search Party Finds Them Same Night

The popular mountain hikes that Principal Macdonald of the Banff Public School, gives his pupils so frequently had somewhat of a set back last Saturday when several of the girls and boys did not obey the wishes of their principal, and hiked out ahead of the party, over Sulphur Square mountain on trails of their own.

Mr. Macdonald is in no way a man for any form in fact but what followed. While purchasing supplies in the Magnet Store he was somewhat surprised when he again reached the store and told that the party had gone on ahead. Three of four of them, he never did see again that day, until he met with Walter Peyto, Ben Woodsworth and several others found Marion and Frances Swanson and Winnie Hatts, somewhere on the south side of Squaw mountain at ten o'clock Saturday evening.

This search party had been organized by Superintendent Stronach and Mr. Macdonald with Ben Woodsworth and Walter Peyto.

It seems that Nancy Brown was one of the lost lambs, but she in her own determined way, struck out across the mountain in a general direction for Banff through snow to the knees and fallen timber, for help, as Frances Swanson was completely played out. Nancy got her message through alright, but many a stronger person would have given up. Nancy was wet through, to say nothing of cold and exhaustion, with her clothes literally in ribbons.

The relief party by lantern light followed Nancy's tracks back and after several hours hiking, found the three girls bedded down for the night under spruce boughs, with their feet wrapped in their sweaters. A fire was at once made and in half an hour's time the party was on the return trip.

Considerable anxiety was caused many persons in town and discreet offered their services to search but it was thought that too many on the mountain would only cause confusion. The careful thought out plans to find the missing girls by the search party deserves credit and too much cannot be said of their wonderful and rapid finding.

To blame Principal Macdonald, in any shape or form, would be most ungracious on his part. There he carefully took to get back to Banff, only to find that no one knew how many were still on the mountain so coming home by the water supply dam. In spite of [illegible] all day hike, Mr. Macdonald went back up to the dam and then again over their tracks of the morning to Forty Mile Creek with the final search party.

Mr. Macdonald has the respect of Banff parents and citizens—this respect he will hold. Fortunate indeed in Banff school to have a man of Macdonald's sterling character and calibre at its head.

The girls who had been lost all turned up for school on Monday morning and apparently suffered no ill effects from their adventure.

CARD OF THANKS

The parents of the girls who were stranded on Squaw Square mountain last Saturday evening wish to thank all those kind folks who helped in the search and gave their aid in bringing them right home, also to Miss Nancy Brown who furnished the search party with information which led to the subsequent discovery of the lost girls.

A story about Nancy Brown's brave rescue of the three lost girls on the front page of the *Crag & Canyon* in Banff in 1925.

The lost girls
Nancy Brown
Banff, October 17, 1925

I don't want Halloween to come to Banff this year. I've had all the fright I need for one October, thank you.

Every time I think about Saturday, I shiver as if I've seen a ghost. Not the ghost that lives in the attic of the Banff Springs Hotel. No, my own ghost, and the white ghoulish faces of Marion and Frances and Winnie, lost in a blizzard on the mountain.

We could have frozen to death up there. I'm too mad at those girls to forgive them yet.

Winnie started all the trouble. Or was it Marion? Or was it Frances? I think it was Winnie.

We had just set out on our Saturday morning hike with our class. Mr. Macdonald, our school principal, stepped into the Magnet Store to buy matches for our campfire. "Wait on the sidewalk for one minute," he said. Winnie rolled her eyes and tapped her foot impatiently.

"Let's not wait around for that old man," she said. "We could go on our own hike through the woods, and get to the amphitheatre on Cascade Mountain before all the other kids in our class."

I didn't think much of the plan, and I said so.

"He told us to wait for him, and he won't know where we are," I told them. "He will worry about us, and we will get into big trouble."

I didn't think Mr. Macdonald deserved this stupid getaway stunt.

"Oh, Nancy, what a baby you are!" Winnie said. "You are a little sissy, scared of your own baby toes."

"Baby, baby, baby," taunted Marion. "Baby toes."

"Sissy baby," Frances repeated in a mean, teasing voice. "Scared sissy baby wants to wait for Old Macdonald Had a Cow."

"E-I-E-I-O!" they yelled together.

They laughed their heads off, and ran ahead of me down the street. Some other kids followed them at top speed. I trudged behind them, looking over my shoulder for a glimpse of Mr. Macdonald, until we left Banff behind to climb into the woods.

"I know where the trail begins," Winnie boasted. "Follow me."

That was our second mistake.

Marching ahead with her diamond willow walking stick, Winnie began to climb a narrow trail up into the woods. Marion and Frances followed her like mountain goats. I looked around for the other two getaway kids in my class, but they had chosen a wider trail. I couldn't see them anymore.

"Are you going to stand there all day, Baby Toes?"

I heard the three girls giggling, and saw them whispering together. I kept my head down, and I followed them. Up, up, and up we walked.

"We will get to the other side of Cascade Mountain in approximately one hour," Winnie said, as if she were an expert Banff guide, like Jimmy Simpson himself. "I know this trail so well I could follow it in my sleep."

She knew it all right. She knew that trail so well, she lost it thirty minutes after she found it. By the middle of the morning, we were bashing away at spruce boughs as we tried to climb the mountain.

"Let's follow this creek to the other side," Winnie announced. We walked along the creek as it twisted and turned like a snake, leading us deeper and deeper into a dark forest.

A cold wind howled through the canyon, nipping the back of our necks. The sun disappeared behind heavy grey clouds. It began to rain softly, and then harder in sheets, and then the rain turned to sleet, and then the sleet turned into a heavy October snowfall.

Snow in our faces, snow on our shoulders, we struggled through slush and underbrush. We climbed up a hill so steep we had to crawl on our hands and knees, dragging each other up, inch by inch, over rocks and sharp stones.

"I am extremely hungry," Marion said to nobody.

"I am soaking wet to the skin," Frances said a minute later.

"We are almost there," said Winnie, but I noticed her lips were trembling.

About three minutes later, we stopped in our tracks between tall trees. A rocky cliff blocked our way in all directions. Looking down at us from a lodgepole pine, an angry crow screeched, as if to say: "Sissy babies. Scared babies. Go home to your town!"

Darkness fell. It was still snowing, and the wind was blowing through our soaking-wet shirts. We heard a scary noise in the bushes that might have been a red fox or a skunk, but was more likely a grey wolf with fangs or a grizzly bear with long, sharp claws.

Marion, Frances, and Winnie started to wail. They cried so

loudly, and for so long, that I thought for sure Mr. Macdonald would hear them down in Banff, and come running to rescue us.

Unfortunately, he did not.

We waited near the dead-end cliff for an hour—hungry, wet, and weary. Those three girls looked like miserable snowmen, minus the carrot noses and the coal eyes. Their eyes were red from crying.

"We are lost," I said, finally. I thought it was time to admit it.

Winnie looked at me, and for once she didn't disagree. She nodded, and started to cry again. "I'm too cold to move," she howled.

"I will go for help, then," I said. "You make a shelter under those spruce trees. Wrap your sweaters around your feet so you don't get frostbite. Huddle together to stay as warm as you can."

As I walked away, I talked out loud to drown out my scary thoughts.

"Okay, Nancy. Go back exactly the same way you came. Down the steep hill, along the twisting and turning creek, and down the narrow trail to town."

I slid down the steep hill on the seat of my pants. Spruce boughs whipped my face, and jagged stones and rocks tore my jacket and pants. I couldn't see the creek through the heavy snow, but finally I waded right into the icy, rushing water. I kept walking through the creek, slipping and falling many times, until I reached what I thought might be Winnie's favourite trail.

It was too dark to see. For hours I struggled along the path, tripping once and falling flat on my face into the snow.

"Get up, Nancy," I yelled to myself. "Keep going!" I waded

112

through snow to my knees, refusing to think that I might never see Banff or my family again. "One more step and you'll be there," I whispered. I didn't believe my own words.

Suddenly, I saw flickering lanterns through the trees. I heard men's voices, shouting our names. Winn-ie! Fran-ces! Mar-ion! Nan-cy!

"Here I am!" I tried to yell. My voice was so weak and trembling that it surprised me, but Mr. Macdonald must have heard me.

In a minute, he picked me up with a big, warm bear hug. He put a blanket around my shoulders, and gave me a butterscotch candy from his pocket.

"Can you lead us to the others, Nancy?" he said in a quiet voice.

I looked up and saw Mr. Peyto, the Banff park warden, and Ben Woodworth and some other tall men from Banff. They were looking down at me, waiting for my answer.

Oh, no. Not that terrible climb again. I was so tired, but what else could I do?

I nodded.

Turning back, we followed my footprints through the snow, walked back through Forty Mile Creek, and trudged through the pitch-black forest for several hours. I was so exhausted that Mr. Peyto carried me sometimes, and I fell asleep against his shoulder. The men followed me as we climbed up the steep slope to the cliff. At last we found Winnie, Marion, and Frances huddled together under the spruce tree, looking like snow ghosts. They were too cold to talk.

Mr. Peyto built a fire to warm them up. After thirty minutes, we struggled through the snow and back down to Banff—my fourth hike along the same route in one day.

Long after midnight, my parents carried me to my warm bed, and covered me with blankets and patchwork quilts.

"The whole town was out looking for you," my mother whispered. "We were so frightened."

Today, the story of our horrible hike appeared on the front page of the *Crag & Canyon*. The headlines says: "Three Local Girls Lost on Mountain; Search Party Finds Them Same Night."

What about the fourth girl? What about me?

I looked at the story until I found my name.

The newspaper reporter wrote: "It seems that Nancy Brown was one of the lost lambs, but she, in her own determined way, struck out across the mountain in a general direction for Banff, through snow to her knees, and fallen timber, for help. Nancy got her message through alright, but many a stronger person would have given up. Nancy was wet through; to say nothing of cold and exhaustion, with her clothes literally in ribbons."

In another corner of the newspaper, the parents of Winnie, Marion, and Frances wrote a Card of Thanks to "Miss Nancy Brown, who furnished the search party with information which led to the subsequent discovery of the lost girls."

Not bad for the girl they called Baby Toes, eh?

—

What do we know for sure?

On October 17, 1925, Marion Swansor, Frances Swansor, Winnie Harris, and Nancy Brown of Banff wandered away from a Saturday class hike, led by their school principal, Mr. Macdonald.

We know what happened because Banff's newspaper, the *Crag & Canyon*, reported the story in detail on the front page on October 23. Walter H. Peyto, the park warden at the time, also wrote about the search in his diary. He said the men found the girls "scared and cold" late in the evening and returned to Banff by foot at 1:20 AM early Sunday morning. The girls had been lost on the mountain in the rain and snow for more than fifteen hours.

The school principal had searched for them all day and evening, going back and forth along another trail. The girls' parents and other people in Banff wanted to join the search, but Mr. Peyto said he didn't want any more people lost, adding to the confusion.

We don't know whether the three girls teased Nancy early in the day, but we do know she was responsible for their rescue. I was not able to find Nancy Brown or her relatives, or the other girls in this story, and would like to contact them if you know of their whereabouts.

The Simpson sisters.

Simpson sisters skate sideways!

Margaret Simpson, age eleven,
and Mary Simpson, age nine, Banff, 1928

If you're coming with us, fetch your skates. Tiptoe down the hall, okay? Don't step on the creaky third stair. Don't let the back door slam.

Yes, it's dark, but don't turn on the back porch light. We have our flashlights, and the moon is full.

Whatever we do, we can't wake them up. If they knew we were out here at 3:42 AM Mountain Time, they would jump out of bed, and fly down here in three seconds. Dad in his long johns. Mum in her flannel nightgown, with pincurls in her hair.

"Get up to bed, lickety-split!" Dad would say. "You'll be a pair of ice cubes by morning if you don't get inside right now."

"You little monkeys," Mum would say. "And who said you could practise in your costumes out here, anyway?"

Nobody told us we could. Nobody told us we couldn't. We didn't ask permission. We didn't want to put them to the trouble of saying no.

We hatched our plot after supper. Dad was listening to a boxing match on the radio, Mum was reading the *Crag & Canyon*. Our little brother Jimmy was asleep in his bed. It was time to put our plan into action.

First, we sneaked into our bedroom with our skates. Back and forth we went, with other little bundles. Nobody looked up.

We carefully closed our door. We hid our figure skates, flash-light, mittens, snow boots, and toques under our beds. We put a Thermos of hot chocolate and some blueberry muffins inside a pillowcase, and stuffed the pillowcase under the blankets.

Moving quickly, we pulled on our long johns. Then we put on our beautiful velvet dresses. Finally, we yanked our baggy night-gowns over our heads, on top of everything.

We hopped into bed and waited for the big test.

"Are you girls ready to turn out the light?"

"Yes, Mum."

She came into our room to say good night. Can you imagine how hard it is to hug your own mother without letting her know that you are wearing three layers of winter clothing in bed? We must have looked like two Egyptian mummies, wrapped in white flannel, lying in the pyramids. We gulped down our giggles.

"You are going to do just fine tomorrow," Mum said. "All you need is lots of rest before the competition."

That's what she thinks.

We know what we need. We need one last practice.

Now don't you say a word. Just follow the glow of our flash-light. Try not to let your boots make that scrunching sound in the snow. We can pull off our nightgowns and lace up our skates, when we get to those trees.

Isn't this a beautiful rink? Our dad made it for us. He used to joke that he would have to build a skating rink in the middle of the kitchen floor to keep Mum and his two daughters at home.

Long ago, our Mum saw the famous skater "The Great Charlotte" in New York. She made up her mind to learn to skate.

When she married our dad and moved to Banff, she would shovel the snow off the frozen river so she could practice her backward loops and her figure-eights on winter days and nights.

We skated as babies, and that's not a lie. Mum would bundle us up in blankets, and tuck us into a small sleigh on metal runners. Tying on her own skates, she would pull us along the ice to give us the thrill of speed and the excitement of quick roundabout turns.

My dad started to worry that his family would crash through the river ice before it melted in the spring.

That's when he built a rink for us in our backyard. First, he shovelled a big square, piling the snow in four deep snowbanks around the outside. We watched him tramp down the snow on the ground into a thin layer. Every night, as we slept, he poured buckets of water on his masterpiece, and blew on his ice-cold hands to thaw his fingers.

"There you go, Billie," he said to Mum when the rink was finished. "You and the kids can skate on your very own Simpson glacier."

Just as soon as we could walk, Mum gave us skates of our own.

She strapped our feet into those tiny "cheese cutters" with double blades. We took little, jerky steps toward her open arms. We tumbled, we stumbled, we toppled, we plunged. We howled, too.

We skated, and got bigger. Mum laced up our hand-me-down skates, pulling the long laces with a yank, to keep them tight. We played Crack the Whip and ice tag and shinny with the other kids in Banff. We raced, we glided, we circled, we slid. To stop, we had to crash into a snowbank on purpose, throw our arms over it, and give it a hug.

Our first brand-new white figure skates had little picks in the front of the blades, so we could stop in a swirl of snow. We skated two perfect figure eights. We skated backward with our eyes closed. We skated together, arm in arm, pushing and gliding in the same direction. Mum offered figure skating lessons on our rink all winter, not just for us, but for other kids in town. Our toes got used to the nip of winter.

We aren't scared of the cold. We aren't scared of the dark. We are just a bit scared of the competition tomorrow.

That's why we want one more practice. We will spin together in the moonlight as snowflakes dust our velvet dresses. We will skate sideways, and backward, in a dance of figure eights. Maybe a mule deer will come out of the woods, to watch us twirl.

We will carve a giant S into the ice with our skate blades. The S will stand for Skating and Sideways and Snowflakes and Sleepless and Secret and Silent and Simpson and Sisters.

We will be warm in our beds by the time Mum calls us for breakfast. A fresh morning snowfall will cover the S on our ice rink with a white blanket.

Only you and a mule deer will know what is underneath.

— —

What do we know for sure?

Margaret and Mary Simpson delighted the crowd with their first figure skating performance at the Banff Winter Festival in 1928. Margaret was eleven years old and Mary was nine.

The Simpson sisters skating on a glacier.

We can only guess their worries on the night before their first competition. Their father did make them a backyard rink, but their practice in the middle of the night is the imaginary part of the story.

We do know that their amazing skating career began at the winter festival the next day.

Gordon Thompson, a figure skating coach from Saskatoon, watched the girls and was impressed with their talent. After the 1929 festival, he invited Margaret and Mary to skate in Saskatchewan, and later in Vancouver, Portland, and Seattle.

The Simpson Sisters, as they became known, continued to

live with their parents, Jimmy and Billie, and their brother, Jimmy
Jr., in Banff. Dreaming of a life as professional skaters, they took
lessons in Toronto in 1934. Their first big break came later that
year at a skating show in Minneapolis, US, featuring Sonja Henie,
a world-famous Olympic figure skater.

At eighteen, Mary Simpson came fourth in the Canadian
Figure Skating Championships of 1936. The sisters joined touring
ice revues—something like the Ice Capades—and performed all
over the United States and Canada in the late 1930s.

Turning to professional skating in 1937, the Simpson Sisters
wore costumes that looked like Mountie uniforms for part of
their performance. Billed as The Sweethearts of the Canadian
Rockies, they skated in Madison Square Gardens in New York.
One American newspaper reported that "for spectacular skating
they are tops." The headline in the *Calgary Albertan* read: "Banff
Girls Steal Show at New York."

In the summer, the sisters returned to Banff to stay with their
family, but they still needed to practise. Their father built them a
new ice rink up on the Bow Glacier. When he finished his work,
he threw his tools down a deep ice crevasse, and later joked: "They
will come out at the foot of the glacier someday, rusted and battered, and some visitors will say: Goodness! Look at the prehistoric
ice scraper I have found!" Jimmy said his daughters would hike up
the glacier, lace on their skates, and then practice their routines.

Margaret and Mary Simpson earned between $350 and $400
a week as figure skaters during the hard years of the Depression.
This was a fortune at the time. They even skated on special rinks
in nightclubs inside hotels. With their money, the young women

helped their parents build the Num-Ti-Jah Lodge at Bow Lake in Banff National Park. You can still visit this interesting log hotel where the Simpson sisters lived and worked. The mountain above the lake is named Mount Jimmy Simpson in honour of their father, a famous Rocky Mountain guide and outfitter.

A year after the lodge opened, Margaret Simpson died suddenly of complications of her first pregnancy. She was only twenty-four years old, and had been married for only a year. Her sister Mary continued her career, but retired from skating in 1955 to help her parents and brother at Num-Ti-Jah Lodge. Later, Mary married and moved to Fort St. James, BC, where she and her husband and daughter established a machine shop business.

Regina Chiesa and her brothers Nino, Alvio, Pietro, or Pete, and baby
Lucino, or Lucky, at their house in Mountain Park in the 1930s.

Does Santa Claus ride the Blue Flea?

Regina Chiesa, age eight,
Mountain Park, 1932

You might like to know that Santa Claus came to Mountain Park tonight, and I talked to him myself.

He was taller than I thought he would be and not so fat. He had a big, booming voice and snow all over his whiskers.

You don't believe me, do you? You think Santa Claus tumbles down the chimney, and tiptoes through the house with his sack of toys, only when he is sure that the kids are fast asleep.

Well, he might do that in your town. We live in a magical town—the highest town in Canada—so our Christmas Eve is different than everybody else's in the world.

I'm not sure, but I think Santa Claus might come here on the Blue Flea.

Why are you laughing? I don't mean that Santa flew over Mount Cheviot on the back of a little blue flea.

We call our train the Blue Flea. Have you ever heard the story "The Little Engine That Could"? That's our train.

We have no cars up here in Mountain Park, and no road down to the rest of Canada. Two huffing and puffing locomotives pull the Blue Flea up the steep, curving railway tracks into our mountains on Mondays, Wednesdays, and Fridays.

Everybody in town stands on the platform to meet the Blue

Flea after supper. We squint down the railway tracks and listen for the train whistle.

Older boys wait and watch for a pretty girl who might come to visit her cousins. Older girls wait and watch for a young miner who might jump down from the train with a rucksack on his back and a sparkle in his eye. They want to meet a young stranger because they want to fall in love with somebody new.

The funny thing is that when the kids and older people in Mountain Park wait for the Blue Flea, we want to see somebody we already love. We wait to hear a shout: "Hello! It's good to see you again!"

When I see the Blue Flea, I have happy and sad thoughts at the same time. I can imagine my father's big smile when my mother and my older brother, Nino, stepped down from the Blue Flea for the first time. My father had worked hard, digging coal, to raise enough money to bring them from Italy to Canada. They had a happy life here for a few years. First, I was born. Then my brother Alvio. And then the baby, Pietro, or Pete as we called him. But then hard times came. My mother became very sick, and the train took her away from me. She died in the hospital in faraway Edmonton. I was only four years old.

The people in Mountain Park felt so sad for me, they gave me seven dolls to be my friends.

My father could not take care of four little children by himself, because he worked underground in the mine every day. Our neighbours took care of my little brothers, but my father had to send Nino and me to live with the Catholic nuns in the convent at St. Albert.

My brother and I waved goodbye and climbed on the train. We left our mountains behind, and travelled for many hours to reach the huge building where we would stay. For two years, I slept in a great big room with lots of other little girls who had no mothers to kiss them good night.

Sometimes my father and other friends came to visit us. They brought candy to share with the other kids. When they hugged me at the end of the visit, I was so homesick for Mountain Park that my stomach hurt.

My father decided we needed a new mother. He wrote letters to Italy to find the right person. A kind woman from his village, Maria Tumini, agreed to marry him and come to Mountain Park. On the day Maria climbed down from the train, our family began to be happy again.

The Blue Flea brought Nino and me back home to stay. Clickety-clack. We're back!

I loved Maria right away. I don't have to worry. She is here to stay.

My new mother sews soft dresses so I can wear new clothes to school. She washes our laundry and hangs it out on the clothes-line. When black coal dust blows over our white bedsheets and my father's overalls, she carefully washes them again. She washes the floor every night for the same reason.

She is teaching my brothers and me to write words in Italian so we can send Christmas letters to our first mother's family in Italy. *Buon Natale e felice Anno Nuovo.* When my father climbs the hill from the mine bathhouse at the end of his shift, holding his coal-black clothes and his empty lunch pail, my new mother

Regina Chiesa, her mother Julia, her brothers Alvio and Nino,
and her father Pietro Chiesa in Mountain Park.

welcomes him home with a shy smile and strong Italian coffee.

At night, when the winter moon shines over Mount Cheviot,
she tucks me into bed. I call her Mama now. I think she is as happy
as me.

Remember when I told you that our town is magical? Here is
why.

Mountain Park is a town with hundreds of kids in it. We live
together at the top of the world. The blue sky is our roof.

We have everything we need up here. In marble season, at
recess, we play Little Rings, Big Rings, Holey, or Chase in the dust.
We swing around the maypole, flying high, hoping our favourite
teacher, Miss Arbuckle, is watching us.

On summer days, I go exploring with my friends Mary and Gloria Liviero, and Caroline and Mary Kabach. We pick forget-me-nots on a hill called Miner's Roof. I like to lie down in a field of buttercups and find animal shapes in the white clouds over my head, or watch for young deer nibbling on the poppies in Annie Antoniuk's garden. In the fall, we pick a pail of juicy huckleberries to eat on the way home.

The big kids have a Tarzan swing, just over the hill, where they can swing a long, long way over the valley if they don't let go of the rope! The little kids can visit a pet bear called Teddy the Orphan Bear, who lives with Ray Jones and his family at the train station. One day Teddy climbed on the roof with a honey tin, and spilled the sticky stuff all over the station window.

We have more horses than people in Mountain Park, and we don't tie them up. When grown-ups want to go trail riding to Tin Roof Cabin or Ruby Lake, they just whistle for the horses, wherever they might be hiding. We can hike up Mount Cheviot or Mount Davis for picnics and treasure hunts, or we can walk to the ball diamond. My brothers go fishing at Flapjack Lake or swimming at the swimming hole, and then come home to eat because they're so hungry for my mother's spaghetti.

After the last bite of supper, we run out of our houses to play Run Sheep Run or Kick the Can or White Horse or Red Light, Green Light. When the sun sets behind the mountain, we whack at beetles on the telephone poles, or tell ghost stories on the Voytecheks' front porch, or roast potatoes at Mile One Hill—all by ourselves in the pitch dark. The big boys play pool in the basement of the Sunset Café.

Sometimes on summer nights, all the kids have a noisy chivaree outside the house of a young bride and groom after the wedding. We bang our pots and pans, and hoot and holler. The couple come out on the porch, laughing, and throw coins to us so we will go away. We take our nickels to the Summit Café to buy a big dish of ice cream, a banana split, or a sweet treat called a Bellyache.

We always have deep, white snow in time for Christmas. I wake up in our house to the sharp nip of the cold, and run as fast as I can to warm up my bare feet beside the stove. My father gets up at five in the morning to light the stove and keep us warm.

On Saturdays in winter, the boys play shinny all day at the rink. Mr. Liviero takes good care of our rink, and he also tells us jokes as he sharpens our skates. He loves hockey so much that sometimes he borrows the coal train to drive the hockey players to games in other towns in the Coal Branch. Everybody in Mountain Park climbs aboard so we can watch our boys win! We pay fifty cents each for the ride. Some people say Mr. Liviero would be fired from the mine if the big boss found out he took the coal train for hockey trips, but nobody tells on him. Mr. Jones, the station master, is careful to stay away from the train station on hockey nights.

I like to skate and make snowmen, or snow angels or snow houses. When it gets dark in the late afternoon, we slide down the hills between the houses, speeding past the outhouses, over the roads, right down to the mine road, and into the mine yard. Some kids use sleds and toboggans, but we also slide on scraps of cardboard, or we sit on the scooping end of a shovel and use the handle as a steering wheel.

Our priest, Father Louis, walked up the railway tracks to reach Mountain Park in the old days, but now he takes the Blue Flea too. We go to mass at our church, and also to catechism class when the Sisters of Service visit us from Edson. The mine doctor says my name, Regina Chiesa, means Queen of the Church in Italian.

All this month, we practised our carols for the Christmas concert. Miss Arbuckle made us sing it again and again until it was perfect.

I was nervous when I saw all the people in the Mountain Park theatre. The whole town was there. We sang, and then the older kids sang, and then some grown-ups sang. The red velvet curtains opened and closed on the shepherds going to Bethlehem, and Uncle Scrooge and Tiny Tim, and Joe Dutton playing the fiddle.

Finally, a big man on the stage shouted to the audience.

"Ladies and gentlemen! Boys and girls! I have just received an important telegram! Santa Claus has been seen in Luscar, Alberta!"

We were shocked. Luscar is another town in the Coal Branch, not too far away, and we weren't even in bed yet.

A few minutes later, the man shouted to us again.

"Boys and girls! I have just been informed that Santa Claus was spotted at Cadomin with a big sack of toys!"

All the kids started to holler and squeal and shout, because Santa was coming toward Mountain Park, no doubt about it. I was a bit confused. Was Santa riding the train that goes from one Coal Branch town to another? Why didn't he fly here in his sleigh? Maybe the reindeer were too tired to fly up into our mountains, so he tied them up beside the Imperial Hotel down in Edson and fed them sugar cubes so they would wait for him.

Regina's hometown was once the highest town in Canada,
but Mountain Park no longer exists.

I was wondering about this when the man on the stage shouted
again. "A new telegram tells me Santa is at Mile One!"

Kids were jumping up and down, and yelling loud enough to
lift the roof off the theatre. The man on the stage shouted at us
through his cupped hands one last time.

"I've just had a message from Mr. Jones down at the train station! Santa Claus is walking this way!"

A minute later, we heard ringing bells outside in the hall. We
turned around and stared with goggle-eyes as Santa Claus ran
through the door and down the aisle. He stopped and kissed the
ladies—with a great big kiss for Mrs. Lukovich—then climbed up
the stairs to the stage to give the biggest, best toys in his sack to the
kids of Mountain Park.

As I tiptoed toward him, he leaned down to whisper to me that
he was happy I was home again. How did he know that I had been

away? I tried to answer him, but I was too excited to say one word. I unwrapped my gift, and I couldn't believe my eyes. It was just what I had been dreaming about! When I looked up again, Santa Claus was waving goodbye.

My friend and I walked home under sparkling stars. Our boots made a crunch, crunch, crunch sound in the snow.

I listened for the train whistle. By now Santa Claus must be riding away on the Blue Flea. Is he winking out the train window at the big moose who stands beside the railway tracks? Is he counting the snowflakes that fall on our sky-high town? Is he thinking about me and my happiness?

What do we know for sure?
Regina Chiesa Dotto told this story in an interview in the summer of 2007, when she was eighty-three.

Her father, Pietro Chiesa, began to work as a miner in Europe when he was a boy of twelve. In 1908, the young Italian travelled to Canada with his brother, Giuseppe, to find a job in the coal mines. After working in different coal mines for a few years, he walked up into the mountains in 1912 to reach an isolated coal mining camp high in the Nikanassin Range of the Alberta Rockies, at the headwaters of the McLeod River. The first train did not reach the camp until 1913.

This camp grew into the little town of Mountain Park.

More than five hundred men worked hard to build the community from scratch. They brought their families from coal-mining countries all over the world, including Italy, Germany,

Ukraine, Wales, Yugoslavia, Poland, and England. People with different languages, customs, and religions learned to live together and help each other. Other mining communities, like Cadomin, Luscar, and Mercoal, sprang up not too far away. Together this beautiful part of Alberta was known as the Coal Branch—and it soon had lively traditions of its own.

Mountain Park was home to about one thousand people when Regina was a child. Her town stood at the top of Canada, sixty-two hundred feet above sea level, the highest community in Canada from 1910 to 1950. The Blue Flea had to travel very slowly to make its way up through the steep slopes to the community.

Young Pietro liked Mountain Park, but he was lonesome. After a few years, he decided to go back to Udine, his hometown in Italy, to search for a wife. He married Julia Casstelini, and soon the couple was waiting for a baby. Pietro returned to Mountain Park to raise the money to bring his family to Canada. They arrived in 1923, and Regina tells the rest of the story about what happened later. After her stepmother, Maria, arrived in the early 1930s, the Chiesa family welcomed a new baby brother, Lucino, nicknamed Lucky.

Most families in Mountain Park lived in small wooden houses. The first Chiesa house had four rooms and a porch, with a wood stove for heat. Families did not have running water inside their homes, so the girls and their mothers had baths in metal tubs at home, while the boys and dads washed in the mine washhouse. Many families had vegetable and flower gardens. Milk, ice, coal, and groceries were delivered to the houses by the driver of a horse-drawn wagon, usually a man named Mr. Noble.

The little town had a school with about one hundred children in it at a time. It also had a two-storey library, a big store called The Mercantile, a hotel, a café called The Summit and another one called The Sunset, and a theatre that was used for movies, dances, union meetings, and the popular concert on Christmas Eve.

The miners' union—the United Mineworkers, District 18—hosted the Christmas concert, and let Santa Claus know that every kid in town needed a big present, even if it was the Depression.

Like Pietro Chiesa and most of his sons, almost all the men in town worked underground in the mine. Coal mining was dangerous in those days, and families dreaded the sound of three sharp whistles, the signal of an accident down below. Over the years, the miners of Mountain Park dug 6.5 million tons of coal and shipped it out of town on the railway to provide fuel for the rest of Canada.

When Regina grew up, she left school and began to work in the Mountain Park post office for forty dollars a month. She married Bino Dotto, a young man from Cadomin, in 1948. Over the years they had five children, David, Daryl, Linda, Dianne, and Julie, and ten grandchildren.

In April 1949, the mine company closed the underground coal mine in Mountain Park. A few months later, on June 30, 1950, the strip mine closed. All of the families had to leave town. The Chiesa family moved to Cadomin at first and transformed a former hospital into a house. When the Cadomin mine shut down, the young people in the family used the lumber from this hospital to build a new house for Pietro and Maria Chiesa in Edson. They lived a long and happy life there.

Regina and Bino Dotto eventually moved to Edmonton and St. Albert. For many years, Regina worked in the Woodwards store. One day, her favourite teacher, the one she knew as Miss Arbuckle, came into the store to talk about how much she missed Mountain Park.

Regina called her classmates together in 1987, and they met with their teacher for special lunches for many years. Hundreds of former residents of the Coal Branch also travelled from all over North America to summer reunions in Cadomin. The gatherings are getting smaller now as the older people pass on.

You can learn more about life in Mountain Park in some wonderful books, including *Oh, the Coal Branch* by Toni Ross, *Mountain Park Memories* by Mary Lee Salzsauler and Joan Talbot Wegert, and *Mountain Park: Forever Home* by Bob Smilanich and Nino Chiesa, who is Regina's older brother.

"Someone should have left a landmark in Mountain Park," said Regina. "The thing that hurt us most is that they bulldozed our town. There is nothing more that says we were there."

Today, Mountain Park is a ghost town, but you can feel the spirit of its children when you hike through the valley.

"I want people to remember that we had a good life there," said Regina.

She remembers every detail about the Christmas concert in 1932, except the present that Santa Claus gave to her. She knows that she loved the gift. What do you think it was?

Children demonstrating during miners' strike, Blairmore, Alberta, 1932.
GLENBOW ARCHIVES NA-3091-5

Watch out, Mr. Brownlee

Striking coal miners' children,
Blairmore, in the Crowsnest Pass, 1932

Dear Mr. Premier,

We bet you read in the *Calgary Albertan* that some kids in Blairmore want to pay you a visit.

You read that right. We have never been to the Alberta legislature before, but we are ready to walk all the way to Edmonton if we have to.

We are pretty darn mad. You'd better get ready for us.

We will stand under your window and yell until you open the door.

We will race up and down your hallways, and flush all the toilets in your fancy indoor johns.

We will run around your office and make a lot of noise, until your head aches and your teeth rattle like they're going to fall out.

We will crawl under your desk and untie your shiny shoes.

We will stick a wad of gum on the seat of your chair.

You think we're joking? You'd better think again. We will pack a big lunch, and walk out of these mountains and along the curvy road through the Pass. We will bring Coleman kids. We will bring Bellevue kids. A real big crowd.

When kids in the Coal Branch up north hear about our march, they will walk right out of their mountains too. Just you wait,

Mr. Brownlee. Kids from Mountain Park and Cadomin and Luscar will be soon be crawling all over your desk, and making paper airplanes out of your important speeches.

Our shouting will sure hurt your ears.

We don't want to give you a nightmare, but maybe you should think about this possibility.

If you want us to stay home where we belong, you'd better end this Depression by next Tuesday, or else.

We are sending you a chunk of coal as a warning.

See you soon, Mr. Brownlee.

Yours truly,
Some strikers' kids in Blairmore

What do we know for sure?

This is an imaginary letter. There is no record that children in Blairmore in 1932 ever wrote to the premier of Alberta, John Brownlee.

We do know that some children in Blairmore marched through their town that year with signs that said they were ready to walk to Edmonton to tell the government about big trouble in their town.

They were the children of some frustrated coal miners.

The Depression of the 1930s was so hard on the people of Alberta that they called this time the Dirty Thirties. For about ten years, everything went wrong. In cities and towns, many parents lost their jobs, and others earned too little money to feed their

Coal miners's children during strike, Blairmore, Alberta, June 18, 1932.
GLENBOW ARCHIVES NA-54-4401

families. After years without enough rain, many Alberta farm families had to walk away from their homes, because no crops would grow.

Families in the Crowsnest Pass and the Coal Branch had a tough time too. They had come to the mountain towns from mining countries all over the world, to search for a better life in Canada. Miners dug for coal in dangerous underground tunnels where explosions, cave-ins, and fires often killed or injured men. It was hard work, but miners needed jobs.

In the 1930s, many Alberta coal mines closed. Others stayed open, but hired only a few miners every day. Sometimes the companies hired English miners first, and turned away immigrants from other countries. Without enough work, many families did not earn enough money to feed their children properly, or dress them in warm clothes. One father in Blairmore said he brought home just ninety cents in two weeks.

In February 1932, the coal miners in the towns of the Crowsnest Pass went on strike to protest for a better deal. By March, one thousand miners had walked off the job. They did not expect much higher wages. They demanded a fair way to divide the work so that everybody could earn a living. The mining company hired unemployed men to take their place. This created bitter feelings in the towns. Many Blairmore families were angry with each other.

The strike lasted for seven difficult months. Many Blairmore children—but not all of them—marched to the mine and around the town with picket signs. City newspapers reported that Communist leaders in the miners' union, and frustrated parents, were telling the kids what to do.

The *Edmonton Journal* reported: "Youths, many of them mere tots, paraded to the homes of the moderates, and were taught to boo by their adult leaders." A police report told the government about "the education of children into Communist propaganda."

Some Blairmore miners said their children understood family troubles well enough to make up their own minds about what to do.

You will have to decide the truth for yourself.

Top of Burgess Pass.

June Mickle
1998

June likes to paint horses in the mountains, sometimes to create her own
Christmas cards. This is one of her later cards.

The girl who painted horses

June Reutin, age sixteen,
west of Turner Valley, 1936

I can't remember when I started to draw horses. I rode them for years before I tried to paint them.

When I was little, I would look at Blondie and Dagwood in the funny papers, and try to copy the comics with a crayon on a scrap of paper. A friend of my mum's gave me a little tin box of watercolour paints. This winter I am painting horses and sleighs on small Christmas cards. I will sell them to our neighbours to earn some spending money.

I live far away from everybody my age. I don't have to go to school, because the nearest high school is too far away. I don't have any brothers or sisters, so I have figured out how to have fun by myself.

I ride horses all day up here. After supper, I sit beside the flickering light of a candle or a coal oil lamp, and draw pictures of horses.

I was born in the month of June, 1920, which is how I got my name. I never knew my real father. He was a soldier who marched away to the First World War, but this is not where he died. A short while after he returned to Canada, he was killed in a hunting accident in Alberta. Last year, when I was fifteen, my mother decided to get married again. She married a cowboy named Tip Johnson, who is a real character.

Tip wears a battered cowboy hat, an old plaid work shirt, blue jeans that look about a century old, and soft leather boots caked with mud. He doesn't own a ranch, or much of anything, but he rents a place up in the hills, where he trains horses for ranchers.

"Well, gal, you're goin' to live in a fine place at the tail end of nowhere," he told me. "There isn't any school, but you'll find friends. We'll get you a fine horse."

On moving day, we rode west toward the mountains, up past Turner Valley, and up again toward the forest reserve.

"Our house is up ahead," Tip said. We strained our eyes, but saw nothing except prairie grass and rising hills. After riding about four miles past the tail end of nowhere, we caught a glimpse of an old log cabin on a bare slope.

The closer we got, the rougher that cabin looked.

My mother and I poked our heads inside the door. The front room had a wood stove. When we stepped on the floor, the wooden boards creaked. You could see daylight through a few cracks in the log walls.

We entered a dusty kitchen where the food was kept. I opened a door that led to a dirt cellar, and sniffed the musty dampness below. This place didn't look one bit like home, but I didn't say a word.

Tip looked sideways at my mother's face. I could tell he was waiting for her to say something.

"Well, let's get to work," she said calmly.

For the first few months, my mum and I worked full-time to fix up that cabin. First, we scrubbed the floor with soap and lye water that took the skin off our hands.

We brought some cardboard boxes up from Turner Valley and

carefully cut them into flat pieces. We nailed the cardboard pieces to the inside of the log walls. Then we tore strips from old bedsheets, dipped them in a homemade glue of flour and water, and smoothed the cloth strips over the cracks between the cardboard pieces.

"Time to paint!" my mother said. We opened little packets of calcimine powder—a kind of cheap paint that cost only ninety-eight cents a box—and we mixed it with water. We painted one bedroom pink, another blue, and the living room walls a nice buff colour.

That was just the start. Mum nailed apple boxes together to make kitchen cupboards. I sewed curtains from flour sacks. We cleaned the privy outside, and tried to find an easier way to haul water from the natural spring about a half-mile from home.

I am always busy here, even if I don't go to school.

In the summer, I pick saskatoon berries and strawberries with Mum, and help her weed her garden.

In the spring, Tip and I ride on horseback to help the ranchers settle their cattle for grazing in the forest reserve. We haul salt for the cattle, and watch that the little calves don't get lost.

In winter, I split firewood and haul it by toboggan to the house. I shovel a path through the snow to the wood pile, then to the privy, then to the chicken house, and then the barn. I milk the cows, bring the milk into the house, and run it through the separator to skim the cream from the milk.

I am teaching a little calf how to drink from a bucket. I stand over her, put my little finger in her mouth, and gently guide her head into a pail of milk and calf meal.

Tip and I ride on horseback into the forest reserve to cut

firewood. Our team of horses pulls the logs home through the snow. When we got home last night, my mother surprised us with homemade bread, beef stew, and hot biscuits. She patched Tip's long underwear as I sketched horses at the table beside her.

"We're running out of coal oil," Tip said last night. "You will need to use candles for a bit. Can you see all right, June?"

I can see all right. Aside from the Christmas cards, I have a few other ways to make my own money. I set my own trapline, but so far I haven't caught any animals. Tip also needs me as a helper. Ranchers pay him ten dollars for every horse he can train to accept a rider. Tip taught me how to ride without getting scared, how to calm an unhappy horse, and how to coax a stubborn one to accept a saddle.

He has star-quality horses, too. A farmer from Okotoks sent us a big brown horse to train, but every time we sent it back, it bucked the farmer again. I worked with that horse three separate times, and I would have done anything to keep him.

I learned how to harness the Pinto to the old stone boat—not a real boat, but a kind of open sleigh on runners—so we could haul water in barrels over the snow. Any time I am a bit lonely, I climb on a Pinto and ride over the hills to visit our neighbours.

In the coldest days of winter, old Dan the Irishman takes a horse and sleigh through deep snow to get grocery lists from our four faraway neighbours. I ski along beside him. Then we ride into town and bring back sacks of flour, sugar, tea, and some hard candies for everyone.

I made skis from the wooden strips of an old barrel. They worked okay, but soon I got a second-hand pair from an old man in Turner Valley. Sometimes I ski all day to a dance in a country hall twelve miles away from home, and then ski home the next morning, just for the fun of it.

I am happy here. I am learning what I want to know.

I can sit with a sketchbook inside a warm cabin as a winter blizzard pushes snow against the door. I can watch an antelope run across the far horizon on a summer night. I can ride as far as any horse will take me. I can sketch and paint the story of my own free life: horses, foothills, mountains, snow.

What do we know for sure?

June Reutin Mickle told this story of her teenage years in a conversation at her kitchen table in Cochrane, Alberta, in 2007.

"I loved it up there," she remembered. "I didn't care at all about what I was missing. All I wanted to do was live in the open country. I was happy where I was."

When June was an older teenager, a friend gave her some oil paints. Another young neighbour, Jack Lowe, took her to visit his friend, who had more oil paints. She allowed June to use them to see if she had any talent. She did, and soon she bought her own paints.

When June rode to the Calgary Stampede every summer, she often went by herself. Once she rode to a town alone to watch a long movie called *Gone With the Wind*. "I ran out at intermission to give my horse some oats," she said. "We didn't get home until 2 AM."

One day during the Second World War years, June decided to

ride by herself to the Dog Pound rodeo, about a hundred kilometres away from her home, just for the adventure. After her first day of riding, she stopped at the Mickle family's place, where she had been invited to stay. She played cards with the family that evening, and noticed that a handsome young son, "as shy as the dickens," was watching her. His father, Charlie Mickle, gave her a car ride to the rodeo, and when she returned for her horse a few days later, the young man, Bert Mickle, told her: "I am going to marry you." This surprised her a bit.

Fortunately, Bert loved horses as much as June. They married and soon had a son, Don, and a daughter, Faye. June has spent most of her life living in the mountains, or near them.

As the years went by, June continued to paint beautiful oil paintings of horses in the Rocky Mountains. Almost every wall in her home carries one of her paintings or horse sketches. In recent years, June has been losing her sight, and she has more difficulty drawing and painting now. Her friend, Kathy Forest Calvert, has been writing her life story.

War evacuees in Banff, 1940: Beryl Hyslop, age nine, with
Peter Haskins, John Gorrie, and Colin Gorrie.

My war in the mountains

Beryl Hyslop, age nine,
Banff, 1942

Let me tell you this. This is no holiday for me. I did not come to live in your Rocky Mountains because they are beautiful.

Nobody gave me a choice. Grown-ups sent me here to keep me alive.

"You will be safe in Canada, Beryl," my teacher told me. "The war will be over soon, and we will bring you home."

She was wrong about the war. It didn't end soon. I have been living here in Banff for two years, and I still can't go home. I blame my homesickness on Mr. Hitler. He started this bad war, and sent German planes to drop bombs on us in England.

I was seven years old then, and I didn't know anything about wars.

One morning, the headmistress at my school, Miss Haskins, asked me to come to her office. What could this be about? I knew I hadn't done anything wrong.

Miss Haskins gave me a hug and started to talk in a slow, quiet voice.

"It isn't safe for children here at Brooklands School, or anywhere in England," she said. "We know the bombs will be coming soon. We have decided to send as many children as possible to Canada."

"Isn't there a war in Canada too?" I asked.

"Yes, in a way, but Canada is safe from attack because it

is so far from Europe, and across the Atlantic Ocean," said Miss Haskins. "Canadians are sending soldiers and food parcels to help us. They are offering to take care of English children, too."

The headmistress told us that her sister, Mrs. Greenham, ran a place called Mountain School in Canada. It was just like an English school, and I would feel right at home.

"You will cross the ocean by ship with dozens of English children," she explained. "When you reach Canada, you will climb aboard a train and travel for many days to reach the Rocky Mountains.

"You will live at Mountain School in a small town called Banff with three other English children—my nephew, Peter Haskins, and John and Colin Gorrie. I expect you to help the littlest Gorrie boy from being too lonely. He is only four."

This trip sounded as scary as Mr. Hitler's bombs. I imagined that the Dominion of Canada would be as cold as an icebox. I started to shiver, just thinking about it.

"Don't worry," said the headmistress. "I am sending my sister Minnie to take care of the four of you until you reach Banff." She hugged me around the shoulders again and gave me a booklet about Mountain School.

The booklet was full exciting promises: tennis, cricket, hockey, horseback riding, skating, skiing, and tobogganing.

How about tobogganing? "It's like sledding," said Miss Haskins.

The booklet also said we would study wildflowers and animals on mountain hikes. We would eat and sleep at the school, like in England.

I read the list about what to pack:

4 sets of underclothes
a pair of stockings
tunics for school wear
a warm coat for winter [navy blue]
a sweater in school colours
a simple white frock
rubbers or overshoes
house shoes
tennis shoes
outdoor shoes
1 dressing gown
gloves and mitts
one handkerchief
a table napkin ring
2 laundry bags
1 shoe bag
toilet requisites, soap, etc.
shoe cleaners
mending requisites, needle and thread
comforter or rug
tennis racquets
skates, skis
rucksack

A few weeks later, I stood with Peter, Colin, and John at the dockside. We waited to climb aboard a huge ocean ship with all the other children. I saw parents and teachers behind a gate, waving and trying not to cry.

The trip to Banff lasted forever, and I won't go on about it. I don't recommend travelling across an ocean and a giant country of trees and flat places in wartime. The trip was scary, exciting, boring, and fun at different times. Some kids were seasick. Some kids were train-sick. All of us were homesick, but we were also curious about our new home.

When I finally climbed off the train in Banff, it was nighttime. I could see the huge, black shapes of mountains against the sky. Many people smiled and hugged us to welcome us. Colin and John stayed close beside my coat, as if they thought those Canadians would bite them. Peter talked to a reporter from a newspaper. Then Mr. and Mrs. Greenham took us home to Mountain School in their motorcar, and tucked us into bed with a big hug for each of us.

Canadian kids speak English in the strangest way—with a flat sound that made me laugh at first—and they use different words. They say flashlight, not torch. Cookie, not biscuit. Yard, not garden. Candy, not sweet. Trucks, not lorries.

We say: "Hullo! How do you do?"

They say: "Hey, there! How's it goin'?"

Mrs. Greenham gave me a little Brownie camera and a notebook for my sketches. I like to make lists in my notebook too.

Things I Love about the Rocky Mountains
Chasing marmots
Elk and deer wander through town

Bears visit the garbage dump
Sunny summer without much rain
The nice smell of lodgepole pines
Mrs. Greenham's dance class
Getting our picture taken with a Mountie
Horseback riding
Acting in plays for the Merry-Go-Round Theatre

Things I Don't Like about the Rocky Mountains
They eat odd bacon
Too cold outside in winter
Grown-ups who ask me if I miss England
Not enough letters from my family
Frozen toes in skates
Scratchy wool hats that make my hair flat
Snowballs down my neck
When Colin or John or Peter gets sad
Too far from Sussex, England

I forgot to put Mrs. Greenham's picnics on my list of favourite things.

One day this summer, she took us to a picnic place beside the Bow River, and I began to chase marmots all over the place. This little brown marmot scooted into the woods, up and down holes, squeaking at me to follow him. I ran after him. Soon I found out I had run quite a long way from Mrs. Greenham and the other kids.

I decided to stay by myself a little while. I had a smart idea

Students from the Mountain School preforming
a play in Banff in the early 1940s.

WHYTE MUSEUM OF CANADIAN ROCKIES M451/7 PDI-14 #3

for a picture. I hid in some tall grass with my camera, and waited
for the hiding marmot to pop up again and run across the rock
in front of me.

"Hey, there! How's it goin'!"

I looked up in a hurry. A young man with blond hair was
smiling down at me. He didn't look scary or mean, but I was a bit
frightened because he was so tall. He looked about twenty years
old. He wore a blue shirt and farmers' overalls, and he was carry-
ing a heavy shovel.

He looked at my camera, and said: "Do you like photography?"

I thought this was a foolish question. Wasn't it obvious if I was lying on my stomach taking pictures? I sat up and stared at him.

He tipped his hat, and introduced himself. "My name is Abe. I come from Rosthern, Saskatchewan. I'm here to fix this little bridge over the creek."

I told him my name, and said I came from Sussex, England.

"I'm here because of the war," I said.

"Me too," he said.

I didn't know what he meant. His voice sounded Canadian, not English, so why did the war send him to this peaceful place? He turned his face away from me for a minute, shielding his eyes from the sunlight with his hand as he looked up at Cascade Mountain.

"I saw you chasing the marmots," he said, turning toward me again.

"We have an animal a bit like that where I come from. We call them gophers, but they're smaller. When I was your age, I chased gophers all over our farm. We didn't want our horses to get a hoof caught in a gopher hole, so we tried to catch them, but they would always disappear into their little homes in the ground. My little brothers are probably chasing gophers this minute."

I looked at Abe's tanned face. He looked just as homesick as me. He pulled a chocolate bar out of his pocket and gave it to me.

A minute later, I heard Mrs. Greenham calling my name, a little bit anxiously. I shook Abe's hand, said goodbye, and ran through the woods to catch up with the other kids. When I got back to the school, I told an older Canadian boy in the kitchen that I met a man from Saskatchewan, fixing a bridge beyond the picnic ground.

"You talked to a conchie?" he said. He rolled his eyes to the ceiling to give me the message that I was the silliest English girl in all of Canada. Maybe even a traitor to the King. I didn't know what I had done wrong.

"What is a conchie?" I said.

"A conchie is a man who doesn't want to be a soldier," he said. "My dad told me not to talk to them."

That night I pulled Abe's chocolate bar from a hiding place under my pillow. I thought about marmots and prairie gophers, running to get home, until I fell asleep.

What do we know for sure?

Four English children—Beryl Hyslop, Peter Haskins, John and Colin Gorrie—arrived at Mountain School in Banff in early August of 1940. Like thousands of other English children, they had to leave their homes and schools to live in a safe place until the Second World War ended.

I tried hard to contact these four English war evacuees, or their families, to ask for their true stories, but I was unable to find them. If they are still alive, I hope they will understand why I imagined parts of their story so that readers would know about their brave trip to the Rockies.

Beryl and the three boys made their long journey at a dangerous time. A few weeks after they arrived safely in Banff, a German submarine torpedoed another ship, the *City of Benares*, which was on its way to Canada with English child evacuees. Of the ninety English children on board, seventy-seven were killed.

The four English chilḏen received a warm welcome at Mountain School.

Margaret and Henry Greenham ran the school as headmistress and headmaster from 1920 to 1947. Born in England, and educated at Oxford and Cambridge, they created a traditional English school in Banff for many Canadian children.

When the war began in Europe, Mrs. Greenham contacted her sisters, Edith and Elizabeth Haskins, who ran Brooklands School in Crowborough, Sussex, in England. The Greenhams offered shelter to their nephew, Peter, and three other children, for the rest of the war.

People in Banff did their best to make the children feel at home. Do you remember the boy in the snowshoe race in the story "The great snowshoe leap"? Peter Whyte was a grown-up artist by the time the English children arrived in Banff, and he was married to another artist named Catharine. This generous couple had no children of their own.

Peter and Catharine Whyte quietly paid the Greenhams to support little Peter Haskins's school expenses, and they gave all of the children many gifts, including cameras, skis, and books. They also loaned a lot of money to the Greenhams so that Mountain School could stay open during the war.

More than thirteen thousand English children were evacuated from their country during the Second World War, and many came to Canada. Beryl, Peter, Colin, and John went home when the war ended in 1945.

Peter Haskins wrote letters to the Whytes for many years, and he came back to live in Canada when he grew up.

Beryl Hyslop was about twelve years old by the time she returned to England. She was living on Napoleon Road in Twickenham in 1992 when she identified photographs of Banff's war children for the Whyte Museum and Archives. She had taken some of those pictures with her own Brownie camera as a little girl.

There is no record that Beryl ever met a man like Abe. This is the imaginary part of the story.

Hundreds of men like Abe did come to the mountain parks in Alberta during the Second World War.

Like Beryl, they had no choice. These Canadian citizens had refused to become soldiers to fight in the war, or serve the military in any way. Many were Mennonites, Hutterites, and Jehovah's Witnesses—peaceful citizens who have a strong religious belief against fighting or becoming soldiers. The Government of Canada allowed these men to avoid military service, but forced them to leave their families and join work camps in the mountains.

They worked hard, forty-eight hours a week for fifty cents a day. They built trails, roads, bridges, and ditches, and cut huge supplies of firewood, in the Rockies. They also planted more than one million trees in British Columbia.

The men called themselves "conscientious objectors" because their conscience objected to war. Other Canadians often treated them badly, and called them "conchies." If they left the work camp, the RCMP would arrest them and bring them back.

English children and conscientious objectors were not the

only people who lived, without a choice, in the Rockies during the war.

The Government of Canada also forced twenty-three thousand Japanese Canadians in British Columbia to leave their homes and go to prison camps. These men, women, and children had done nothing wrong. The Canadian government treated them like enemies because Canada and Japan were at war.

Hundreds of Japanese Canadian men were forced to build a stretch of the Yellowhead Highway through Jasper National Park in the Rockies. They lived in rough work camps. Many years later, Canada apologized to the Japanese Canadians for this mistreatment. You can visit one place where they lived, and read the Canadian government's statement of regret, at a historic site just west of the town of Jasper.

If you go to Banff, Jasper, Kananaskis, Waterton Lakes, or Yoho National Park to camp in the Rockies, you may walk on a bridge, or drive on a road, built by the conscientious objectors or the Japanese Canadians. You might even chase marmots on a trail that was explored by a peaceful girl named Beryl in the middle of a terrible war.

Downhill, head first!

Kathy Forest, age sixteen,
Lake Louise, 1963

I own the ugliest skis in the world. One look at those old sticks, and you would probably warn me not to risk my life on them.

After the first snowfall this year, I decided to learn how to ski. My dad was just starting his business, and he told me: "Kathy, if you really want a pair of skis, you will have to save your money and buy them yourself."

I searched for the cheapest second-hand skis in the city of Calgary, and I found a bargain. They cost fourteen dollars.

They are old wooden skis, battered and bruised. One is red. The other is blue. I painted them white to make them look a bit better, but the paint is peeling off. The beat-up bindings are a mess. Ski boots? I lace up old leather boots, push my feet into the tangled bindings, and grab the creaky poles to keep my balance.

Here's the surprise. I went skiing with the Canadian National Ski Team on those crazy skis last weekend.

It was almost a downhill disaster, but I'm getting ahead of my story.

I have loved the mountains for as long as I can remember. When I was little, we lived in Edmonton, but we spent summers on my grandparents' farm. My dad started to take me hunting and fishing when I was two, and I was always begging to go with him. I made my first winter trip when I was six.

After that, if my dad ever saw me in a gloomy mood in the city, he would say: "If you cheer up now, I will take you to the mountains in the spring."

He kept his promise. My mum liked to stay in the city, so my dad took my sisters and brother and me camping and hiking on the warmer weekends. Once we visited an old man who worked high up in a fire tower, watching for forest fires with his binoculars. He served us hot chocolate. We watched a pigeon hawk and listened to his stories of brave crews fighting the summer flames.

When I was twelve, my family went on a summer camping trip through Jasper National Park, Banff National Park, and as far as Glacier National Park down in Montana. I tried mountain climbing for the first time on that trip. I liked the earthy smell of the spruce woods in the mountains, and the sparkle of cold streams in the canyons. A magpie followed us and became our pet.

It was cool up high. The wilderness felt like my friend.

When we moved from Edmonton to Calgary, I found a new friend, Karen Taylor, who was already a ski racer. She wanted to join the Canadian ski team, so she practised every weekend in Banff and Lake Louise during the winter.

"You should come with me," she said. "You would love the speed."

So I bought my wacky skis, and then faced the next challenge. How could I afford to go to Banff? My allowance is only five dollars a week. Karen's mother said she would be happy to drive us both to the mountains every Saturday if I would bring a loaf of my mother's delicious homemade bread for our lunch. "It's a deal," I said.

Every Saturday morning, we pack up our ski equipment, drive

into the mountains, and rent a little upstairs room at Mum Lindo's boarding house in Banff. When Karen and I are really broke, we wash her floors and she feeds us.

I loved the idea of downhill ski racing from my first minutes on the slopes at Norquay. My big problem? I didn't know how.

Last Saturday, just after we arrived at Lake Louise, Karen grabbed my arm and whispered: "Look! There's Nancy Greene and Scott Henderson! They must be training here today!"

We tried not to gawk as we watched Canada's most famous skiers walk past us to the chairlift. All of the team members seemed tall and strong, and a lot older than us. Nancy Greene smiled at us with her famous Canada-wide grin. She looked even friendlier in person than she did on TV. We scrambled after her, and Karen started talking as soon as she looked our way again.

Karen was already a pretty good skier. She felt at ease with the racers. I was still a newcomer to the sport, and it was a struggle for me just to keep them in sight. I still had trouble turning or stopping when I was going fast.

At the end of each practice day, the team members would ski as fast as they could down to the bottom of the steepest run. Then they would line up to watch their teammates ski the course.

I rode up the hill on the chairlift without saying a word. When we reached the top of the slope, I let everybody else go first. Team members crouched down on their skis, and with a *whoosh*, they raced down the hard-packed slopes at the speed of light.

Karen murmured words of encouragement to me. In a whisk of spraying snow and sunlight, she zoomed down the hill after her heroes.

I was alone, a frozen girl on wooden planks. I clenched my hands inside my mittens. Shivering in the wind, I looked down at my battered boots, my beat-up bindings, the red ski, the blue ski, and the peeling paint as white as all the snow in the Rockies.

I looked up at the high peaks. I looked down at tiny specks of human beings, skiing this way and that way, like the confident Olympic champions on TV. I realized I wanted nothing more in the world than to get down the hill in one piece.

Well, here goes nothing!

Down I went. Straight down. Head-first down. Luckily, not upside-down.

Everywhere I looked, frightened Albertans were scrambling to avoid a determined Calgary girl hurtling down the hill on two flat boards that looked like old canoe paddles.

Down at the bottom of the hill, the Canadian ski team—their eyes wide with alarm—stared up at me. As my speed increased, I realized that if I tried to stop, I would hit the line of skiers like a bowling ball. In a flash of inspiration, I remembered the huge snowbank that lined the hill access road, just beyond them. I thought I was going fast enough to fly off the snowbank like a ski jumper, clear the road, and keep going.

I raced past Karen with my ski poles flying. I zoomed past Scott Henderson too quickly to admire his handsome face. I whizzed past a shocked Nancy Greene at top speed.

On those old wooden skis, I flew over the huge snowbank and went soaring through the air: a pigeon hawk without wings, a magpie in old leather boots, a screech owl without a screech left in her.

Suddenly, with a huge *whump*, I crashed into the snowbank. I was not going nearly fast enough to escape the muddy road below.

Blue sky turned to black.

I don't remember what happened after that. Later, Karen told me that everyone hurried after me, yelling for help. "She's unconscious!" somebody shouted. "Don't move her!"

When I woke up, I was staring into Karen's terrified eyes. My body hurt all over, but I had only one question for my best friend.

"Did I break my skis?"

— —

What do we know for sure?

Kathy Forest Calvert told this story in a conversation in 2007. She and her friend Karen really did go skiing with the Canadian National Ski Team, and Kathy ended the race in the snowbank on her old skis just as the story described. She wasn't badly hurt, and her old skis survived too.

In the 1960s, Canadian kids looked to the members of the national ski team as heroes. Nancy Greene became Canada's top ski racer. She earned gold and silver medals at the 1968 Grenoble Olympics, and her thirteen World Cup victories remain a Canadian record. Calgarian Scott Henderson won three Canadian men's titles, but he is best known for coaching the famous Crazy Canucks ski team to great victories in 1975 and 1976.

As an older teenager, Kathy Forest continued her mountain adventures with challenging back-country ski trips with the

Alpine Club of Canada. Once, she climbed to the top of Emerald Pass, through deep powder snow. Sometimes she was the only girl on these trips.

Through high school, Kathy and Karen continued to go to the Rockies for hiking, climbing, camping, and skiing. Like many teenagers, they worked as hotel chambermaids or store clerks so they could stay in the mountains.

When she was twenty-six, Kathy supervised a wilderness Conservation Corps for girls between the ages of fifteen and seventeen at Waterton National Park. In 1975, she became one of Canada's first female park wardens at Yoho National Park. During her long career as a park warden, Kathy participated in the first all-women's expedition to Mount Logan in 1977, and the first all-women's ski traverse of the Columbia Mountains from the Bugaboos to Rogers Pass in 1989.

She earned a Master's degree in environmental science in 1994, and developed a new system to deal with garbage in national parks, still in use in Jasper. Her husband, Dale Portman, was a dog handler and rescue worker for Parks Canada. Kathy retired from the national parks service in 2000, and has turned to a writing career with her husband. She is the author of *Quest for the Summits*, the life story of her mountain-climbing father, Don Forest, the first person to climb all eleven-thousand-foot peaks in the Canadian Rockies and Columbia Mountains. She also co-wrote *Guardians of the Peaks: Mountain Rescues in the Canadian Rockies* with Dale in 2006.

Kathy Forest Calvert lives in Cochrane, Alberta, in the foot-hills of the Rockies—not too far from her favourite ski slopes.

Sara Renner, a future Olympic champion, skiing in the 1980s.
COURTESY OF THE RENNER FAMILY

Sara's daydream
Sara Renner, age twelve,
Mount Assiniboine Lodge, 1988

Jump! I dare you.

Don't be scared. I'm right down here with my brother, Andre, and my sister, Natalie. If you tumble into a snowdrift over your head, we will scoop you out in fifteen seconds.

No, we don't have shovels. We will dig you out with our mitts.

If you can climb to the top of a tall tree, with all of those scratchy branches poking your face, you can fly through the wide, blue sky into the snow.

You can do it. I know you can do it.

Take a deep breath. Stretch out your arms. Close your eyes, and pretend you are soaring from the top of Mount Assiniboine into the biggest, softest feather pillow in the world.

You did it! Do you want to climb back up the tree, and try again?

Jumping from trees into snowdrifts is just one of my favourite things to do up here.

In the summer, we like to go hiking and camping in the back-country—just Andre, Natalie, and me—without our parents. Jenn-Cat follows us for three days without a meow of complaint. We aren't scared of grizzly bears one bit, and she isn't either. We can pitch our own tent, cook our own food, make our own fire, and take care of ourselves —although the strangers we meet on the trail hardly ever believe it.

When winter comes, we like to build a snow cave near the lodge, and sleep in it overnight. My dad ties "pieps"—avalanche receivers—around our necks so we can feel like real adventurers. We already know how to make a safe snow cave, and how to judge if the avalanche danger is high when we're skiing, and what to do in an emergency.

Sometimes I like to ski in the woods by myself, watching for elk and listening for grey jays. I like to build tiny rescue huts for rabbits. I fill old yogurt containers full of water and nuts, and put out the little huts in places rabbits visit.

When we get hungry, we run into the lodge to see if Trudi has pulled a tray of steaming-hot chocolate-chip cookies out of the oven.

"Want some?" Trudi says, as if she had to ask the question

"I guess so," I say, as if she didn't know the answer.

With the taste of melted chocolate in our mouths, and warm cookies in our pockets, we go outside again to ski on Ellie's Dome—up and down, up and down—through a perfect afternoon. We don't need ski lifts, lift tickets, snow from machines, or slopes packed as hard as pavement. All of these things belong to the world down below.

We climb Ellie's Dome on our own skis in big, jerky steps, slipping backward, pushing up and up and up until we lose our breath. Our skis make giant V shapes in the snow as we climb. I guess the V stands for Very Exhausting Effort. When we are too tired to climb another step, we turn around slowly, and . . .

Swoop! Down we go through deep, powder-soft snow. *Whoosh!* Our skis carve long, graceful ribbons in the hillside behind us. *Swerve!* We poke our ski poles into the crust of each snowdrift, pushing forward, kneeling for speed.

Sometimes the lodge guests watch me and my brother and sister, gliding toward the log buildings, and I can tell they are thinking: "Were those kids born on skis?"

Not quite, but almost. All Renners and MacGougans are born to ski— the kids, our parents, aunts and uncles, cousins, grandparents, and even our distant relations. My father, Sepp, grew up skiing in the mountains of Switzerland. My mother, Barb, grew up skiing in the mountains of Canada. When they met at Stanley Mitchell Hut in the Rockies, they decided they wanted to ski together for the rest of their lives. I think they got married so they could raise three kids to ski beside them wherever they went.

I was born in a mountain town with a beautiful name: Golden. When I was a baby, I would bob along in a backpack, looking up at birds, as my parents skied through the woods. I took my first steps on tiny skis of my own at Mica Creek when I was two or three years old. From that day on, I could hear my mother whisper to me in a soft voice, "You can do it, Sara. Just slide one ski in front of the other. I know you can do it."

We moved into Mount Assiniboine Lodge just before Christmas, when I was seven years old. Andre was nine. Natalie was five. We ran around the old log buildings together, exploring every dusty corner. My parents unpacked food and sleeping bags.

"This is how we will make our living," my mother explained.

"We will guide the skiers through the mountains, teach them about the wilderness, feed them delicious food, and give them a safe place to sleep inside this lodge. We will send them back down the mountain happier than when they climbed up. What do you think?"

The three of us thought we had arrived in heaven.

It was an ice-cold heaven at first. On the first night at the lodge, the temperature plunged to minus forty degrees. I'm not kidding. My parents built a huge fire in the wood stove. They put foam mattresses on top of the dining room tables. Then they tucked us into our sleeping bags on top of the mattresses, and pulled our bed-tables closer to the warmth of the crackling fire. When we woke up in the morning, our foamies were frozen to the tops of the tables.

"Maybe this old lodge should be torn down," the government people told my parents. "It is in bad shape. If you think you can fix it up, and welcome skiing guests from around the world, you are welcome to try."

My parents worked hard to repair the lodge and fix the nearby log huts. They wanted the lodge to look like a comfortable home in the backcountry, not a big, fancy resort hotel.

On Mount Assiniboine, we have no indoor toilets or bathtubs or electric lights or television or hamburger joints or bubblegum machines.

What we do have is mountains.

We are way up amid the peaks of the Great Divide, the high ridge of the Rockies that separates Alberta and British Columbia. There are no roads up here. To get here, our guests have to ski or

Sara grew up skiing on Mount Assiniboine.
COURTESY OF THE RENNER FAMILY

hike along a twenty-eight-kilometre trail that twists and turns all the way up to the lodge. When our family is in a hurry, we ride by helicopter back and forth to Canmore.

An old Norwegian skier, Erling Strom, took care of Mount Assiniboine Lodge for about fifty years before our family arrived. He left many mysterious signs behind for us to figure out. He made a symbol for the lodge—broken ski poles—and he hand-painted the doors with unusual designs. Maybe Erling wanted to bring a bit of old Norway to Canada.

My mother carefully explains to newcomers that there are no bathtubs. Guests can take a shower in the shower hut, or enjoy an outdoor sauna, or my father can bring a pail of warm water to their cabin in the morning for washing.

Everybody eats together at big tables. Our guests talk about skiing or hiking adventures as they gobble down Trudi's famous raspberry chicken. After a blizzard, we peek out of windows at a world of snow. On those days, our lodge can feel like a snow cave. We sit on handmade chairs that were made of wood and elk hide a long time ago.

Our family sleeps in a cabin near the lodge. My parents built three bunk beds into a tiny room the size of a closet, and that became our bedroom. When we were little, we would fall asleep on the chesterfield beside the wood stove in the lodge. Later my parents would carry us to our family cabin, and put us into their big warm bed to snuggle and stay warm. Late at night, they would say good night to the guests, and move us into our own bunks so they could go to sleep.

I keep my shoes on the top bunk to throw down at Andre!

We can go out skiing whenever we like. We don't need ski lessons from a stranger.

"Just watch me, and try to do this," my father says. "It's called telemarking."

With his heel free, he kneels down and skims through the snow, leading with one ski and trailing the other one behind. This is how you turn when you're in deep snow, high on the mountains, back and forth, all the way down. My father is a professional ski guide. He can make anything look easy.

Telemarking is like balancing on a tight rope. A circus in the snow. When I tumble sideways into a snowdrift, my father grins at me, gives me his hand, and pulls me back to my feet.

"Try again, Sara," he says quietly. "You can do it. I know you can do it."

Sometimes, at the end of a weekend around the lodge, we ski all twenty-eight kilometres down to Canmore in one long, twisting line of family and guests. It would be easier to take off our skis and walk, but it's funnier if we don't. There are so many switchbacks, and so many ways to fall, that we end up laughing our way down to town.

I am happy to report that there is no school on top of the seventh tallest mountain in the Canadian Rockies. Up here, it is pure freedom.

Every September my mother takes Andre and Natalie and me down to Canmore to live in a regular house so we can go to school. My father stays with the guests up in the lodge, and waits for us to join him on the weekends, school holidays, and through summer vacations.

Waiting isn't always easy for me. I am not a sitting-still type of person. I am a moving-around type of person. You know what it's like to sit at a desk on a Wednesday afternoon in winter? A kid can feel like a trapped marmot in school.

Sometimes I can hardly hear my teacher's voice when she talks about the Charter of Rights and Freedoms, or Canadian trade with China, or how many Great Lakes there are in Canada. When she starts to mumble about how to draw angles in geometry, or how to divide big fractions into little fractions, her words just drift away to the ceiling.

My mind is on another kind of math. I call it daydreaming math.

I am counting the minutes—sixty-five minutes —until my next ski race.

I am counting the hours—seventy-two hours—until I can climb into a whirring helicopter and fly over the deep canyon, over Bryant Creek, over a landing strip near Lake Magog, to my true home at Mount Assiniboine Lodge, where Jenn-Cat will be purring a welcome.

I am counting the days—fourteen more days—until the fastest ski racers in the world arrive in Canmore to compete in the Winter Olympic Games.

On that beautiful day, I will be somewhere in the crowd, with all the other Renners, cheering the Canadian skiers as they race toward the finish line.

"You can do it!" I will shout to them at the top of my lungs. "I know you can do it!"

What do we know for sure?

Sara Renner discovered a new daydream on the day she cheered the cross-country ski racers at the 1988 Olympic Games in Alberta. The twelve-year-old began to imagine that someday she would be an Olympic athlete too.

At fourteen Sara started racing in competition as a cross-country skier. She competed in her first Olympics in Nagano, Japan, in 1998, and placed in the top twenty in each of her events at the Olympics in Salt Lake City in 2002. She skied in World Cup events in skiing countries around the globe to prepare for her triumphant Silver medal victory in the 2006 Olympics in Torino, Italy.

That last race delighted Canadians, but scared them first. Sara was sprinting toward her teammate Beckie Scott at top speed in the relay race when her left ski pole broke. "It was like being in a canoe with no paddle," she said later. "I was in shock." Suddenly, a man named Bjornar Hakensmoen, the coach of the Norwegian ski team, handed her another ski pole. She was able to reach Beckie, who skied extra fast to make up for the lost time, and they won the medal.

Everybody in Canada loved everybody in Norway that day.

After the race, Sara remembered a strange coincidence. Hadn't it been another Norwegian, Erling Strom, who had taken care of Mount Assiniboine Lodge for fifty years before her family took over the job? And hadn't that old man left behind the symbol of the broken ski pole for the lodge? The memory made her smile.

Sara married Canadian alpine skier Thomas Grandi, who has won two World Cup gold medals. Now thirty-one, she hopes to

Olympic skiers Beckie Scott, left, and Sara Renner with their medals.
COURTESY OF THE RENNER FAMILY

compete in the 2010 Winter Games at Whistler, BC.

The Renner family has run Mount Assiniboine Lodge with loving care for twenty-five years. Built in 1928, the oldest ski lodge in the backcountry of the Rockies is located inside Mount Assiniboine Provincial Park, and is owned by the government of British Columbia, and managed by the Renners.

"This is the beautiful place where I grew up, and it has defined me as a person," Sara said in an interview for her childhood story. "It has given me my strength."

On February 1, 2007, her mother's birthday, Sara gave birth to a baby daughter, Aria. The baby has already enjoyed a ski trip near Mount Assiniboine Lodge, looking out at the beautiful mountain peaks from a warm backpack on her mother's back.

Ryan James in the 1990s.
COURTESY OF THE JAMES FAMILY

A quinzhee in Kananaskis Country

Ryan James, age eleven,
Lower Kananaskis Lake, 1996

Thirty below zero, Centigrade. That's cold, right?

Have you ever slept outside in the Rocky Mountains on a winter night when the temperature dipped to minus thirty?

Well, I did it last weekend. I huddled inside a snow hut with Lance, Eric, Cody, Ben, Jason, and a few other friends of mine. I am happy to tell you that I still own all of my fingers and toes, and the rest of me is in good shape too. No frostbite. No pneumonia. No nightmares. No kidding.

I have to say that summer camping is a lot easier.

I'm in Scouts. Every spring and summer, we take our gear out to the Scout Lease beside the Bow River, a good place between Canmore and Exshaw. We play Capture the Flag, and hike up rocky trails on sunny days. We cross creeks on stepping stones and rocks, or over a log bridge that we cut with an axe. Sometimes we discover islands and play tag on them all day. Sometimes we spy on beaver as they build their lodges beside the river.

At night we roast corn on the cob, and bake potatoes, burgers, and veggies in tinfoil over the hot coals in the campfire. For dessert, we roast marshmallows and eat s'mores like there's no tomorrow.

When I turned eleven, I was ready for a winter adventure.

My dad is a Scout leader, so he had already told me about the possibilities.

"Winter camping is lots of fun, Ryan, as long as you know exactly what you're doing," he told me on the night before we left. "You will have to learn to build a quinzhee, but that's not too difficult."

After school on Friday, about eight kids drove out to the campsite with our Scout leaders, Mike, Alex, Richard, and my dad. We played Fox and Hares in the snow for awhile, and then pitched tents where we would sleep the first night.

"Okay, everybody," said one of our leaders. "We need to get started on the quinzhee. Grab a shovel and start digging. We have to create a giant pile of snow before we can eat our supper."

Have you ever built a quinzhee? This kind of snow hut does not look like an igloo at all. If I built an igloo, I would carve blocks of snow and carefully pile up the chunks in a circle. A quinzhee is quite quirky. It begins with a stack of snow about two metres high, and about three metres wide in a circle.

"Find a soft place with no big rocks or bumps in the way," said another leader. "Heap the snow up high, but don't pack it too tightly."

We shovelled snow until our elbows ached, but for some reason, it was more fun than shovelling a sidewalk or driveway after a snowstorm at home.

Quinzhee shovelling is quicker, but we were hot and sweaty after all of that heavy lifting.

Our Scout leaders looked carefully at the giant snow heap we had built.

"That looks great!" my dad said. "Now we will leave the mound alone so the snow will settle down overnight, and the outside surface will harden."

We waxed our cross-country skis, and followed snowy trails into the deep, dark woods. The trails were steep and tough to climb, but so much fun to slide down on the other side of a hill. Branches touched my face, and I could hear hooting owls in the woods. I wondered if a moose or even a wolf might be watching me from a hiding place. At least the bears would be fast asleep, hibernating in a snow hut of their own.

In Alberta, we get used to darkness in the late afternoon in early winter. When we were hungry and tired, we skied back to our campsite before the light disappeared behind the mountain. We huddled around the wood stove inside the picnic shelter, sipping hot chocolate and warming our feet beside the crackling fire. We ate steaming mounds of Mountain Spaghetti for supper, with chocolate-chip cookies for dessert.

The ice-cold wind nipped my fingers as I ate. I moved closer to the wood stove to keep warm. Looking at those thin tents in the snow, I shivered. I wasn't looking forward to sleeping outside through a long night that already felt like the inside of the freezer in our refrigerator at home.

Our leaders warned us about our clothing as we got ready for bed.

"You can't sleep in your snowpants or heavy coat or snow boots, because you will sweat too much, and that could lead to hypothermia," one said.

Hypothermia sounded horrible. I decided not to get it.

Inside the tent, each Scout claimed two sleeping bags. I stuffed the first one inside the second one, and then I crawled inside both of them. I wore long underwear with heavy socks on my feet. I pulled my wool toque over my ears, as far as it would stretch. Curling up inside that double sleeping bag, I listened to my friends' whispers and tried not to think about horrible hypothermia, or coyotes, or that deep pile of snow, the quinzhee, that would be our home on Saturday night.

O Canada, the true north, strong and freezing. I was so cold that night I couldn't bend my knees. My kidneys turned to ice cubes.

I woke up to the sound of the chattering teeth of eight Scouts. Clickety-clickety-click. I could see my breath when I peeked out the top hole of the sleeping bag. With a groan, I stood up and pulled on layers of clothing for the day ahead. My fingers were blue icicles, and they wouldn't bend at the knuckles, so each layer of clothing was more difficult for my frozen hands than the one before. My toes pinched me with cold. I pulled on my heavy coat, yanked on my snow boots, and headed outside into a snowdrift.

I raced to the cooking shelter to warm up my hands over the wood stove, so that I could zip up my coat.

After one mug of hot chocolate and a hot breakfast, I felt happier. The sun was bright, and the snow deep and clean. We went snowshoeing all morning, following the curve around Lower Kananaskis Lake, through meadows and bushes.

"Okay, time to go back!" a leader shouted after we had snowshoed about three kilometres along the trail. "Our quinzhee should be ready for digging by now." We turned around and headed for the campsite.

The second part of making a quinzhee is to hollow out a room on the inside. Slowly and carefully, we dug a tunnel into one side of the snow pile for an entrance. Then we scooped out the inside cave with a shovel, and pulled out the extra snow through the entrance tunnel. We were careful to leave thick walls and a ceiling for warmth.

We piled the leftover snow on top of the hardened roof of the hut to create an extra layer of warmth.

Then we crawled back inside the snow hut. We lit candles inside the room to melt a thin layer of the walls. We let the candles burn for a few minutes, then we blew out the flame. The melted layer froze again into a final coat of hard ice. Now we knew the ice walls and ceiling would be safe enough for us.

"We're almost finished," said a leader. "I'll poke a hole in the roof so we will get some fresh air inside."

I was worried our hut would fall apart, but it didn't.

That night, after supper, we crawled into the quinzhee. I knew right away that it would be much warmer than the tent had been the night before.

Outside, a cold wind howled through the lodgepole pines, and the temperature plunged again to minus thirty. Inside the quinzhee, we were cozy and comfortable in our sleeping bags. We told jokes in the glow of our flashlights.

The best part of winter camping? Tasting the melted chocolate of my last s'more of the night, and feeling warmth come back to my toes and fingertips as I fell into a deep winter sleep. When

I woke up in the morning, sunlight shone through the roof and turned the walls of the quinzhee to a beautiful glacier blue. I looked up at the snow ceiling, warm and happy.

—————

What do we know for sure?

Ryan James did build a quinzhee on a winter camping trip with his friends in Scouts in 1996, when he was eleven years old. "It was like a big adventure, very exciting," he remembers.

Ryan was born in Canmore, Alberta, on June 25, 1985. He grew up in the nearby mountain community of Harvie Heights with his brother, Shaun, his mother, Karen, and his father, Brian, who became a leader in the local Scouting movement as soon as his sons joined for fun.

Boys and girls can join Beavers at age five, then Cubs or Brownies when they are eight years old, Scouts or Guides when they are eleven years old, then Venturers and Rovers when they are older. Ryan enjoyed all aspects of Scouting, but especially canoeing and camping in the mountains. In 2007, the Scouting movement celebrated its one hundredth anniversary around the world.

Ryan's family lives in a comfortable house in Harvie Heights, surrounded by mountain spruce and pine trees. As he looks out the living room window, he can count thirteen mountain peaks, including Mount Rundle and Ha Ling Peak. He can watch many birds and animals from those windows too.

Ryan is now twenty-two years old. His most recent adventure was a backpacking trip to Australia and New Zealand, where he made sure to visit the mountainous areas. He has a dog named Zeus, and he still loves camping in the Rockies.

Quinzhee huts, also called snow-mound huts, must be made carefully to be safe. The snow can collapse if the weather is too warm. Build them only on very cold days when you have a parent or other grown-up nearby to help. You should also keep a safety shovel handy to clear the snow.

To learn more about Scouts in Canada, go to the website www.scoutscanada.ca

Eric McDonald and Bailey Wanyandie in 2007.
COURTESY OF THE MCDONALD FAMILY.

Friends in high places

Eric McDonald and Bailey Wanyandie,
Grande Cache and Wanyandie Flats, 2007

My friend Bailey is one of the luckiest kids in Canada. How many friends do you know who get a real bow and arrow for their eighth birthday?

The other day, I heard my dad saying that he was driving up to Wanyandie Flats to visit Bailey's family. I didn't want to miss that. That house is full of things I like to look at.

"Can I come along and see Bailey?" I asked.

"No, Eric," he said. "Not today."

Who gives up after one no?

"Please," I said.

"No, son," he said. "Not today."

"Could I please go? I want to see Bailey."

My dad could tell I wasn't going to give up and stay home. He smiled at me and said: "Okay, okay. Climb in the truck. We're on our way."

We rode along the Big Horn Highway on our way to Bailey's place in Wanyandie Flats. Dad let me use his digital camera so I could take pictures of deer and elk through the window. "Hey, look up there," he said, pointing up to a high cliff. "See those three white spots? Those are mountain goats." He slowed down so I could take more pictures.

My name is Eric McDonald. I live in Grande Cache, Alberta, a high-up, beautiful town in the middle of forests and mountains. I am nine years old and in Grade Four. I live with my mum and dad and my brother, Stephen, who is eleven.

Can you see mountains where you live? If I look out our windows at home, I can see Mount Louis, Stearn Mountain, Lightning Ridge, and Grande Mountain. People are cutting down a lot of trees to build new houses in our town, but it isn't too big. I like Grande Cache because you hardly ever hear police sirens or ambulances. We have deep snow in the winter, and yellow leaves to walk through in the fall.

I play soccer and baseball with my friends at school, and sometimes I go swimming at the rec centre. I also go fishing with my family. We bring milkshakes, sandwiches, and granola bars to Pierre Grey's Lakes, and we eat and we wait. I caught a rainbow trout once, but my dad said I had to put it back in the water. That trout was lucky.

You would love Grande Cache in the winter. I play road hockey with my brother, or go sliding on the icy road. My brother and I take our Crazy Carpets to go sledding down a big hill behind my house. Some Saturdays, we take our shovels into the yard and fill the wheelbarrow full of snow, over and over again. Then we dump all the snow to make a huge hill—not quite a mountain, but pretty big—and we pack it hard with our mitts.

Have you ever made a snow fort? It is more fun with a high pile of Grande Cache snow. You can climb up to the top of a snow hill, and push your brother down. You can slide down on your stomach. You can push the hill over, and build it up again. If you stand on top, it is a perfect place to throw snowballs.

In my yard, I also like to write words in the snow with my boots. Sometimes I write the names of my cousins. Other times I write words of animals I like. Bear, elk, or deer. My favourite animal is the sabre-toothed tiger and my favourite bird is the golden eagle, but that might be too long to write. Dad says I can only write snow words in our yard, not in other people's yards, so I always run out of space.

Grande Cache can be icy cold in the winter, but not all the time. I wear my navy jacket on top of my regular clothes, and then I put on snow gloves, a toque, and snow boots. I get dressed up even warmer if we go snowmobiling. Last winter, in the mountains, the snowmobile got stuck, and we all had to dig and dig with sticks to get it unstuck. If it is too cold and windy outside, I stay inside and play with my Game Boy, or watch hockey or cartoons on TV.

Visiting Bailey Wanyandie is up at the top of my list of Things I Like to Do.

My dad and I turned off the highway and followed a road through the trees.

As soon as I saw the horses, I knew we had reached Wanyandie Flats.

—— ——

"Hi Eric!" said Bailey. I think he had been waiting for me. We took our shoes off and left them near the door.

Bailey is eight, and he's also in Grade Four. He lives with his mum and dad and his brothers and sisters, Justin, Rebecca, Faith, and Abigale.

Inside the house, Bailey's dad was working on a deer hide in his workshop. He makes things from nature as a hobby. That's why my friend's house is full of amazing creations.

You probably know that large animals in Canada, such as moose, elk, caribou, and deer, have antlers they use to protect themselves. The animals shed their antlers after they mate. Bailey's Dad finds these antlers in the woods—he calls them "sheds"—and he brings them home to his workshop. Many people bring antlers to his house to help him. Bailey's mum knows what to expect when she opens the door. She is very patient.

Bailey's dad carves the shapes of animals—bear, deer, elk, hawks, moose, and eagles—inside the antlers. He also makes many things for the family's house.

"Let's go to your bedroom, first" I said to Bailey.

"Sure," he said. His brother Justin led the way. Their bunk bed is made from a spruce tree. It isn't one of those shaky metal bunk beds from a store that wiggles when you climb the ladder. The peeled logs are strong enough to hold all of their toys in the top bunk. Bailey has a Batman blanket.

We played with their light sabres for awhile, and then Bailey and Justin showed me their parents' room. We had to be quiet because Abigale was asleep on the big bed.

"Look at this," whispered Bailey. He pulled open the dresser drawers with handles made from deer antlers. Bailey's dad has made all of the furniture in this house from spruce logs: the beds, the dressers, even the big kitchen table and chairs.

We walked slowly from room to room. I saw carvings of an elk, an eagle, and a mountain lion inside antlers. Justin showed me his video games and a big TV. Bailey showed me an old bow and arrow on the wall. "My dad started making these when he was our age," he said. "He makes the bows from wood soaked in water so that it will bend. He carves the arrow tips from a moose leg bone."

I saw a beautiful framed box full of medicine plants: willow, cedar, sage, and sweetgrass. "That's my mother's favourite," Bailey said. "She says it makes her happy to see it."

On the wall I saw a huge painting of three people on horseback riding up a mountain trail.

"My sister Faith stands on the couch and tells the story of all the things that happen inside my dad's painting," Bailey said. "She finds things in the picture, like a rabbit, that nobody else can see."

It was almost time to go. I asked Bailey to show me his favourite treasure in the house.

He stopped to think. First, he pointed up to the ceiling. Over the kitchen table, little lights shone inside a huge lamp made of twelve antlers from moose, elk, and deer.

Bailey led me to the closet in his parents' bedroom. "That's my bow. We keep it here for safety. My dad made me a practice target behind the shed. Maybe you can try it the next time you visit me."

On the way home to Grande Cache in the truck, I aimed my camera at all of the wild animals beside the highway. "Some day, Eric, you can have that camera," Dad said.

That gave me an idea. Maybe I could take pictures with my camera the way Bailey's dad makes carvings. I could put up the pictures all over my walls, so kids would want to visit Eric's famous house.

I see an elk. Look at the antlers!

What do we know for sure?

One spring day in 2007, Eric McDonald of Grande Cache did visit his friend Bailey Wanyandie in his interesting house at Wanyandie Flats. I went along too, and talked to them about what they liked best.

Both boys belong to the Aseniwuche Winewak, the Rocky Mountain people. Their families are descended from Beaver, Sekani, and Secwepemc or Shushwap people who lived in the northeastern Rocky Mountains, and from Cree, Iroquois, Nakoda Sioux, and Ojibwa, who came west with the fur trade in the 1700s and 1800s.

Many of these families lived in the Rocky Mountains when the Canadian government created Jasper National Park. In 1907, the government told the families to leave the park and find a new place to live. The families travelled to the Grande Cache area to stay near their relatives. They lived in a traditional way—hunting and trapping, and trading, and living in tipis and log houses, until the 1960s. New people began to move to Grande Cache to work in a coal mine, to search for oil and gas, and to work in the forestry industry.

Eric's town of Grande Cache is growing quickly, and it is now home to forty-five hundred people. Around the town you can see twenty-one mountain peaks and two river valleys. Up the highway, Bailey's community of Wanyandie Flats is much smaller. His father, James Wanyandie, is well-known for his beautiful antler carvings.

Eric does love photography, and Bailey did get a bow and arrows for his eighth birthday.

Rocky Mountain Words
a glossary

Many of the kids who live or travel in the Canadian Rockies speak many languages other than English. Here's a short list of new words used by some of the kids in the stories in this book.

Cree

tân'si—hello

nehiyawewin—the Cree people, one of the largest First Nations of Canada.

pakwatastim—my good horse

nâpemaskwa—a mother bear. A male bear is *maskwa*.

wâpos—a rabbit

Aseniwuche Winewak—the Mountain People, the name of First Nation people of mixed ancestry who live in the Grande Cache area.

Métis

Métis—a Canadian of mixed ancestry, someone who has First Nations ancestors and European ancestors too. *Michif* is one of the languages of the Métis people in western Canada, a mixture of Cree and French.

bannock—a delicious homemade bread, sometimes made over a campfire; tasty with soup or stew.

pemmican—or *pimihkân* in Cree—the main camping food of the fur trade in Canada's early days. A mixture of dried buffalo meat, flour, and saskatoon berries, it was packed in big sacks for long trips across the West.

Red River cart—a cart with two huge, creaking wheels, pulled by horses or oxen; a common form of transportation across the Prairies in Canada's early days. The cart was named after the historic settlement of Red River in what is now southern Manitoba.

French

voyageurs—brave people who paddled the canoes for the fur trade in Canada's early days. They carried heavy packs of furs on their backs during portages. Sometimes they were also called *coureurs des bois*, which means "runners of the woods."

portage—Sometimes the rapids, or quick-flowing places over rocks in the rivers, are so dangerous that canoeists must unload the canoe on the riverbank. Then they carry the canoe and all their belongings on their shoulders through the woods until it is safe to travel on the river again. This is called portaging. In Canada, these stopping places are called portages.

Iyarhe Nakodabi

Iyarhe Nakodabi—the Nakoda Sioux people of the Canadian Rockies, or in their language, the Mountain People. In English, these First Nations are sometimes called the Nakoda, or Nakota, or Stoney Nakoda. Long ago, in historic times, English-speaking newcomers also called their people the Assiniboines or the Stonies.

ade—father

ina—mother

aba washded—good day, or hello

dudiki naca—Where are you going?

hakijhi—tomorrow

Secwepemc Nation

Secwepemc—the First Nation of seventeen bands that claims south-central British Columbia as its traditional territory. English-speakers have also called these people the Shuswap people. To learn about their communities today, go to www.secwepemc.org or www.shuswapnation.org

Ktunaxa Nation

Ktunaxa—the First Nation that claims southeastern British Columbia as its traditional territory. Historically, they also lived in parts of Alberta, Montana, Washington, and Idaho. English-speakers called them the Kootenay people, or the Kutenai. The Kootenay mountains are named after them. To learn more about their communities today, go to www.ktunaxa.org

German

danke schön—thank you

auf wiedersehen—goodbye

mein liebes Kind—my dear child

Italian

Buon Natale e Felice Anno Nuovo—Merry Christmas and Happy
New Year

Old-fashioned or unusual words in English

privy—an outdoor bathroom; also called an outhouse, a biffy, or
a john.

chamber pot—a pot or bowl placed under the bed in the old days
before there were indoor toilets. A chamber pot was used as
a toilet at night when it was too cold and dark to go outside
to the outhouse.

maypole—an old-fashioned playground game. Children would
hold on to the iron bars, and swing on chains in a circle
around a tall iron pole in the centre.

oakum—a sticky, oily material made from old rope; used to fill in
the cracks in boats in the old days.

Quaker—a member of a Christian religious group, also known as
the Society of Friends.

locomotive—the big, front part of a train, where the engine is
located.

chivaree—a noisy celebration outside the house of a newly-
married couple in the old days. Sometimes the bride and
groom would throw coins to the crowd.

whooping cough—an infection of the breathing areas of the body,
causing a bad cough. This was a serious illness among children in the old days, but it is rare now because of immuniza-
tion (the shots you get in your arm to prevent sickness).

shinny—a hockey game played for the fun of it at an outdoor rink, or on a frozen river, creek, or pond. Anybody who turns up can play.

frock—an English name for a dress.

rucksack—the old-fashioned name for a backpack.

hobnailed boots—strong hiking boots used in the old days.

shintangle pudding—Shintangle is a low evergreen bush found in the north woods. And shintangle pudding? I couldn't find the recipe!

Brown Betty—a tasty dessert made of sliced, cooked apples, with layers of bread crumbs and brown sugar in between, and applesauce and butter on top.

fried farina—a camping food in the old days. Farina is a kind of powdery flour, made of grain, nuts, or starchy roots.

Johnny cakes—an old-fashioned American pancake, made of cornmeal instead of wheat flour.

huckleberries—delicious dark blue berries found in the Canadian Rockies in late August.

saskatoons—small purple berries that appear in late July and August. Western Canadians love them! Saskatoons taste a bit like blueberries, and are especially good in homemade pie and jam.

pika—a tiny mountain animal that looks like a guinea pig, but is not related. Pikas have tiny hairs on the soles of their feet to help them hold on to rocks. Listen for their funny "eek" noise near rocks. Pikas are easier to hear than to see.

marmot—a small mountain animal in the squirrel family, with a black line across the nose and black feet. You can hear marmots make a long, slow whistle sound. They dig tunnels and stay in their warm underground homes with their relatives through the long winter. Fun to chase.

lynx—a large wild cat that lives high up in the mountains in the summer, and in the forests during the winter. A relative of other wild mountain cats like the bobcat or the cougar, the lynx almost always stays away from humans.

grizzly bear—A large brown bear with a big shoulder hump and long claws, the grizzly wanders in the high meadows in the summer. Grizzlies eat as many as two hundred thousand buffalo berries a day when they can find their favourite treat. They are good swimmers and mountain climbers, but prefer to sleep through the winter.

telemark turns—a kind of swinging motion in skiing, for turning or for stopping in deep snow.

headwaters—the place where a river begins.

pieps—the short nickname for avalanche receivers. This is an important piece of safety equipment for people who like to ski or snowboard in the backcountry.

the backcountry—the wilderness area of the Canadian Rockies, far away from highways, cars, towns, and tour buses. A wonderful place.

quinzhee—an outdoor shelter made inside a pile of carefully packed snow.

Mountain Spaghetti—any kind of spaghetti you make when you're camping in the mountains. Not too fancy, but it tastes good.

s'mores—a delicious campfire treat, a kind of gooey cookie sandwich. Melt a chunk of chocolate bar and squish it over a campfire-roasted marshmallow, then put the sticky marshmallow between two graham crackers. Try not to let the whole mess fall in the dirt. The name comes from the feeling you get when you've eaten one s'more. You quickly want to eat *some more*.

Sources

For a full list of sources for the stories in *Rocky Mountain Kids*, and some interesting suggestions for further reading, go to: www.brindleandglass.com

Rocky Mounatin Kids is the second in this series. The first was *Kidmonton: True Stories of River City Kids*. Stay tuned for more stories on kids from across Canada, over time.

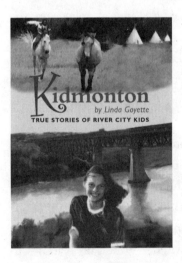

Acknowledgments

I owe my first thanks to the generous storytellers across Alberta who worked with me to adapt their life stories for this book. It was a pure pleasure to listen to them, and I appreciate their help.

The Edmonton Public Library provided a creative place for me to complete the manuscript when I was Writer in Residence in 2007. I am grateful to Linda Cook, the Director of Libraries, and her colleagues for offering firm support to the writers in my city. I value the insights of Alberta's librarians, and their commitment to readers of all ages.

In my research for *Rocky Mountain Kids,* I relied on the thoughtful suggestions and advice of Alberta's archivists. I am especially grateful to Ted Hart, Elizabeth Kundert-Cameron, and Lena Goon at the Whyte Museum of the Canadian Rockies in Banff; and to Doug Cass and Jim Bowman at the Glenbow Museum and Archives in Calgary.

I am also grateful to Sherry Letendre, Liz Letendre, and Tanja Schramm for their careful reading of the Iyarhe Nakodabi stories; to John and Maria Koch for their groundbreaking research on Marcelle Nordegg, their suggestions for her story, and their generous assistance with photographs; to the McDonald and Wanyandie families of the Aseniwuche Winewak Nation; to Jasper naturalist Ben Gadd for sharing his knowledge about the Canadian Rockies; and to Pamela Cunningham, Cheryl and Peter Mahaffy, Kathy Coxson, Colleen Skidmore, and Brian Brennan for ideas that became stories.

I have been fortunate to work on this project with publisher Ruth Linka, a consummate professional who defines the word patience, and her fine colleagues at Brindle & Glass Publishing. I am grateful to editor Lynne van Luven for her helpful advice on the manuscript, and to Christine Savage, the copyeditor.

Finally, I thank my husband, Allan Chambers, for the pleasure of his company on research trips to the mountains—and for his enduring support for my work.

LINDA GOYETTE is an Edmonton writer and journalist with an interest in Canadian history. Her previous books include *Kidmonton: True Stories of River City Kids*; *Edmonton in Our Own Words,* for which she won the Grant MacEwan Author's Award in 2005; *Standing Together: Women Speak Out About Violence and Abuse*; and *Second Opinion.*